Heart
& Soul

AWAKENING YOUR
PASSION TO SERVE

GARY MORSCH, M.D., & DEAN NELSON, Ph.D.

Gary Morsch, MD
September 29th 2004 (signature)

D1465924

Beacon Hill Press of Kansas City
Kansas City, Missouri

Copyright 1997, 2002
by Beacon Hill Press of Kansas City
Second edition, 2002

ISBN 083-411-6812

Printed in the
United States of America

Cover design: Michael Walsh

Photo by: Tony Stone

Library of Congress Cataloging-in-Publication Data
Morsch, Gary.
    Heart and soul : Gary Morsch, Dean Nelson.
      p. cm.
    ISBN 0-8341-1681-2 (pb)
    1. Heart to Heart International.   2. Missions, Medical.
  3. Medical assistance, American.   4. Missionaries, Medical.
  I. Nelson, Dean, 1954- . II. Title.
RA390.U5M67   1997
362.1'06'073—dc21

                                          97-26956
                                            CIP

10 9 8 7 6 5 4 3 2

**To the life and memory of Steve Lamb,
a friend and creative teacher
who taught me the paradox of "thinking small."**

Steve Lamb was on his way to teach his Sunday School class one Sunday morning in 1991 when his car was hit head-on by a drunk driver, as noted in chapter 3. Steve was critically injured but lived five more years confined to a wheelchair as a quadriplegic. He died on June 2, 1997, just as this book was first going to press. Though a tragic accident took away most of Steve's mobility and independence, it did not take away his passion to serve and to teach. Steve always reminded us to think small, that is, to respond to the common needs that are all around us if we have eyes to see.

CONTENTS

HEART TO HEART
MISSION STATEMENT

Heart to Heart International is a global humanitarian organization that inspires, empowers, and mobilizes individuals to serve the needs of the poor in their communities and around the world.

Heart to Heart accomplishes this mission through partnerships that promote health, alleviate hunger, deliver resources, education and hope, and provide opportunities for meaningful service.

FOREWORD

I am constantly amazed at the creativity of people. The world is filled with those who have invented, discovered, uncovered, figured out, and created. In my time as a U.S. Congressman, I have seen some of that creativity unleashed on problems that are simple, and some that are very complex.

Sometimes government can provide an answer to a particular problem. Sometimes other avenues are necessary. Sometimes we simply need a problem solver to figure it out.

One of the problem solvers I admire has found a way to combine the inner desire of every human being with a global need to help relieve suffering. He's not a United Nations ambassador, and he's not an elected official. He's a private citizen—a doctor—who saw a need in a refugee camp years ago and created an organization that now reaches into some of the neediest places in the world.

Gary Morsch believes that everyone has an innate desire and ability to help others. With that simple premise, his organization, Heart to Heart International, has responded to natural and economic disasters in this country and around the world—using volunteers. The United States government, along with many international corporations, consider Heart to Heart one of the preferred groups to go into hard-to-reach areas. They know that where there is a need, in this country or elsewhere, Heart to Heart will find a way to get medical and humanitarian aid to people in need.

And they do it with virtually no overhead. Out of the hundreds of millions of dollars worth of assistance they have provided in their first 10 years, less than 2 percent has gone to administrative costs. In an era where philanthropy is under great scrutiny, this is an organization that has stayed true to its mission.

This is a book that will inspire you. It might not get you working in refugee camps, but it will make you take note of the needs of people you encounter every day. It will awaken in you something you were born with, and are now ready to rediscover—your desire to help one another. Gary didn't discover service to others. He just made it more desirable and practical. When you're done with *Heart and Soul*, you'll be looking for ways to serve. That's the best creativity there is.

—J. C. Watts, Member of U.S. House of Representatives
1995—2003

INTRODUCTION

There is a concept in sociology called praxis. This is the concept that the kind of learning that transforms persons is the learning that is reflection in the context of action. Heart to Heart is very much committed to the praxis concept. Its leaders believe that as people reach out to address the needs of others, things happen that change their own lives dramatically. As they reflect on these changes and try to understand what is taking place in their lives, they learn things about themselves, about others, and about God that can be learned in no other way. I am convinced that it is only through praxis that we can come to grips with what it means to be people of faith. Simply accepting doctrinal statements with all of their orthodoxy is not enough. It is not enough to know God with your head; you have to feel God in your heart. The latter can be done only in the context of living in service to people.

The new humanity cannot be gained in abstract reflection, nor can it be obtained through action alone. Within the context of action one experiences the mystical presence of God, and as one reflects upon that presence, one comes to know the God who is life eternal.

Heart to Heart is an international humanitarian organization that has reached around the world to touch hundreds of thousands of lives. Stories that are told in the following pages will provide not only inspiration but also insight as to how God can be known in a world of suffering. It is the story of people who become grateful in service because they encountered more than people in need when they went to the needy. Heart to Heart will challenge you to do what you can where you are in the midst of those who suffer.

—Tony Campolo

PROLOGUE

There is something about Heart to Heart International that has struck a chord in individuals, corporations, and governments around the world. There was no way of knowing it would be such a success when we first began, but I have to confess that every day I am amazed at the willingness of people to help others.

Sometimes we forget that corporations and governments are made up of people too. But when I see corporations acting in humanitarian ways, and governments putting needs before politics, my sense of why we are all here is renewed. We are created to help one another. It's a message that has resonated from Moscow to Myanmar to Miami. It crosses all political, economic, and religious boundaries.

When we first published this book about Heart to Heart in 1997, the response was overwhelming. In ways we never imagined it could, it motivated and moved people to action. We knew the stories were powerful, because of the way they had impacted us, but we had no idea the stories would connect so deeply with others—people from all walks of life throughout the world. Since the first printing, total strangers have contacted Heart to Heart and asked how they can volunteer in some way, either in their own hometown or on one of our international airlifts. It has been amazing!

While the response to this book has been incredible, the way in which Heart to Heart has grown and changed has also been incredible. As a result of Heart to Heart's success in helping people in need, governments from around the world now routinely contact us when they see a need, and ask how they can partner with us to meet it. In addition, corporations also regularly call and offer their services. Federal Express called us on September 11, 2001, just hours after the attacks on the World Trade Center and Pentagon, asking how they could help relieve the suffering at those sites. They provided transportation for some product needed in NYC as well as an enormous warehouse for us to use in Brooklyn. Our partnerships with individuals, governments, and companies illustrate perfectly one of the principles on which Heart to Heart was founded: People want to help each other—they just don't always know how. Providing opportunities to serve and help is where Heart to Heart comes in.

And this is truly how Heart to Heart started—not as a result of a wonderful plan where a few of us spread maps of the world on a conference room table and declared, "This is how we will do good." More accurately, a few of us just wanted to find a way to help—the idea for Heart to Heart the organization sort of snuck up on all of us.

Long before I went to medical school, I committed to devoting a few weeks out of every year in some kind of volunteer service. Once my medical practice was up and running, I gave some of my time to working as a volunteer doctor in refugee camps, mission hospitals, and inner-city clinics. Each time I would return from one of these missions, a local civic club or school or church would ask me to speak to them about my experiences.

Heart to Heart began with one of those speeches.

During my years in private practice, I was a member of my local Rotary Club. One Wednesday noon I walked in late to our meeting, and before I could find a seat, the club president called out my name. The scheduled speaker had not shown up, and since I'd just returned from several weeks in Vietnam and Cambodia, they wondered if I could fill in and talk about my recent trip. At the conclusion of my extemporaneous comments, I spontaneously challenged the hundred Rotarians in the audience to take on an international project—to literally go to some desperate place in the world and meet a need. As I stepped down from the podium, the club president was waiting. "Dr. Morsch, would you serve as the chairman of a committee to organize an international volunteer project?" I agreed. That off-the-cuff speech changed my life.

Heart to Heart did not begin with a grand strategy. We did not set out to build a world-class relief organization. Heart to Heart began with a small group of ordinary people who had a passion to use their skills and resources to help people in need. The first international project entailed a dozen people traveling to Belize, Central America, and remodeling a YWCA. The next year we traveled to the island of St. Croix and rebuilt a community market that had been destroyed by Hurricane Hugo. In 1991 they were ready for another project. "This time," I said, "let's take on a project that will really stretch us. A project that's much bigger than this club. A project that will require the support of people throughout the Kansas City area."

"What kind of project do you have in mind?" they asked. "Where would we go?"

This was 1991; the Soviet Union was still a strong, threatening superpower. We were in the middle of the cold war and still referred to the USSR as the "evil empire." "How about a project to Russia?" I suggested. "I know they're our enemy. But why not do something really bold, something that will build a bridge of friendship between the people of our two countries?"

So a small group of us traveled to the Chernobyl region of Russia to explore the possibility of a project for children affected by the now infamous nuclear disaster. We were not prepared for what we found. The Russian health-care system was in crisis. The shelves in their pharmacies were bare. The country had run out of medicine and had little money to manufacture or buy more.

We decided to send medicines and medical supplies to Moscow, the very heart of Russia. I'd never tried to get an airplane donated, let alone enough medicine to fill one. We didn't know where to start.

We wanted to send the medicines on Valentine's Day, 1992. That would be quite symbolic, we thought. To Russia with love. From the heartland of America to the heartland of Russia. And so we settled on a name—we'd call it a "Heart to Heart" airlift!

Since that first project more than 10 years ago, we have conducted several airlifts each year to the neediest regions around the world and also worked in more than 30 cities of the United States, providing desperately needed medicines, supplies, and education. And throughout our history we have endeavored to complete our mission efficiently: our organizational overhead is only 2 percent; and because of our partnerships with transportation companies, corporations, and pharmaceutical companies, we are able to leverage every $1 received into an average of $25 of aid delivered for people in need.

Millions of lives have been touched and changed forever because of Heart to Heart—some of the stories of which are recorded in this book.

And just as important, the work of Heart to Heat and the stories in this book have motivated thousands of people around the world to look at their own communities to find ways to serve others.

Early in my medical practice I saw colleagues who were making a living, and others who were making a life. I want to do the latter. Don't you? I think you will when you read this book.

—Gary Morsch, M.D.
President and Founder
Heart to Heart International
Kansas City

———

Gary Morsch and I had just finished watching *The Grapes of Wrath,* the Tony Award-winning production at a Broadway theater in New York. He was in New York for a board meeting for the Lamb's Club, a shelter/resource center/church in the middle of Manhattan, and I was in town to do a project for the *New York Times.* We were both staying at the Lamb's. We had been acquaintances for years.

It was about midnight as we walked back to the Lamb's. Just before we got there, he said, "Let's keep walking for a while."

We walked through the nearby Times Square, mobbed with people and traffic at that hour. Eventually we ended up walking through Hell's Kitchen. It was even more crowded there. Playgrounds caught the light of passing cars, and when they did, the ground shone as if it was covered with diamonds. But it wasn't jewels that were reflecting. Crack cocaine vials that had been ground underfoot were in tiny pieces of glass. Every time a car would pass, we could see a new constellation of crack containers.

The taxis were busy that night too. Bodies of prostitutes had been found in recent days in the motel rooms they usually used.

So, for their own safety, they conducted their business in the backs of cabs. No one was hiding much of anything that night.

That's what we saw. It helped inspire Gary to talk about his vision.

"Wouldn't it be something to be able to match up people and their talents with other people and their needs?" he asked. "What if, after a hurricane, for instance, you could just call on people who were carpenters or contractors and get them together with the people who needed those skills?"

For the next few hours we walked through needy parts of town and talked about the best way to identify and motivate people to help relieve the suffering of each other.

That's Gary. Always thinking about angles for meeting needs.

It's no surprise to me that he came up with the idea of Heart to Heart International soon after. It matches his interest and ability as a medical doctor with specific needs of people around the world. But it also matches people's deep desires to have a purpose in their lives with that very purpose: to love God and others.

Most of the world is amazed at what Heart to Heart has accomplished in providing so much help to so many people. What amazes me more, though, is how it cuts across every conceivable human barrier in providing a means for people to discover why they were put on this planet.

I conducted hundreds of hours of interviews to write this book; and while some details varied from one person to another, they all had a similar message: My life has meaning, now that I am purposefully working to help others.

The entire book is written from the point of view of Gary Morsch. But it is the same point of view you'll find in every person I talked with. Writing this has made me far more conscious and intentional about the world around me. I trust it will do the same for you.

—Dean Nelson, Ph.D.
Point Loma Nazarene University
San Diego

1

ANOTHER FINE MESS

IT WAS A STANDOFF. I KEPT LOOKING AT THE PILOTS TO see if they were backing down, and every time I did, their resolve seemed stronger. Grim-faced, tight-lipped, they slowly shook their heads.

We were all tired. It had been a long flight to Moscow, and the lines of fatigue that ran through our faces and clothes creased our brains as well. There seemed to be no solution.

The C-5 cargo plane sat on the tarmac of the Moscow airport, and its exterior acted as an oven, transforming the sun's rays into heat to bake the inside. And inside were the two pilots and me. Overheating. Arguing.

"Why not?" I pleaded for the 10th time.

"They are members of the Soviet army."

"So?"

"That's answer enough."

I didn't care much for politics at the moment. It was only getting in the way of doing what needed to be done. The Soviet Union hadn't dissolved yet; it was still considered *the enemy.* The pilots and I were arguing about letting the enemy board the plane to help us unload it.

This wasn't what I anticipated for this day, but given what else had gone wrong already, it was consistent. We had started this flight to Moscow from the Rhein Mein Air Base in Frankfurt, Germany, after flying in from Dover, Delaware, the night before. We were on a tight schedule. It was the first flight into Soviet airspace for these pilots and crew members. They wanted to get to Moscow and unload quickly so they could leave while there was still daylight. They were determined not to get caught on the ground with darkness coming.

Early that morning we had climbed aboard that huge aircraft, started the engines, and waited for clearance to take off for Russia. Then we were told to wait on the tarmac. There was a problem. After waiting for more than an hour, I hadn't been able to stand it any longer—I wanted to find out why we weren't moving. I got permission to get off the plane, and headed for the airport's operations center. It seemed that more political posturing was getting in the way. Latvia had refused to grant rights to fly over that country. This meant we would have to prepare and file a brand-new flight plan and get new overfly rights from other countries.

It was a mess.

On our flight was a member of the U.S. Joint Chiefs of Staff, and he decided to telephone the Department of Defense and the secretary of state in Washington, D.C., to see if someone could put pressure on the Latvian government to change their minds.

Meanwhile, the pilots had been getting more nervous as they watched the sun climbing in the sky. Would we have time to fly to Moscow, unload, and fly out before nightfall?

I had assured them that everything was under control, but my pulse was racing.

Finally, after four hours of tense negotiations at the high levels of our governments, permission was granted, and we took off. We flew over Latvia without incident, although I kept looking out the window for a Russian MIG to intercept us. We were in Soviet airspace. What a feeling to sit in a U.S. military plane, looking down on Soviet territory! The pilots weren't enjoying it, from the looks on their faces. As we neared Moscow, Russian air traffic controllers started radioing us—first in Russian, then in broken English. Finally we were cleared for landing.

I had been sitting in the cockpit between the pilot and copilot. I could see that they were sweating. Would the unloading equipment be ready, they kept asking? Will we get back in the air before dark? I had assured them that everything was under control, but my pulse was racing. We were about to land a C-5 in Moscow.

We landed. And then we waited. A Russian soldier came on board to officially check us. Then we were allowed to get off the plane.

The big moment arrived as the ground crew brought up the equipment to unload the plane. The great nose of the plane came up. The tail came down.

And then the unloader had broken.

We had transported 160 pallets of medicine and medical supplies worth $5 million on this plane, destined for hospitals, burn centers, and other clinics that were experiencing desperate shortages. The pallets filled the C-5, which is one of the largest cargo planes in the world. There are only 130 of these planes in existence. Only a few airports in the world are built with enough support to allow them to land.

Now it was late afternoon, and I was wondering if we were going to have to turn around and take off without having even taken these supplies off the plane. The pilots were ready to close the nose cone, refuel, fire up the engines, and leave right then, regardless of their fatigue and my begging.

Before we ever left Washington, we had arranged for equipment such as forklifts, trucks, and conveyors to meet us at the Moscow airport to remove the pallets and transfer them to several large trucks. We could then take the medicine to the hospitals and clinics full of sick and dying patients who were suffering from the effects of massive shortages.

Our group of volunteers had been working on this airlift for more than a year. The medicines and supplies were in the country, only a few miles from their ultimate destination, but it looked as if it would all unravel. The only way we could get the material off the plane now was by hand. There were about a dozen people in our delegation. Taking the equipment off box by box would take days.

Standing right outside the plane, though, were hundreds of

Russian army cadets. They were willing and eager to help. But the pilots wouldn't allow it because it would mean allowing them to enter a U.S. plane.

"It's enough that we had to fly into Soviet airspace," one of the pilots complained. "But I draw the line on letting Soviets step into my aircraft."

The thought of flying a clearly marked U.S. military plane into the enemy's capital gave the pilot and copilot reason to let their imaginations run wild. Was this a trap? Were we tricked into coming here so they could take us and our aircraft hostage?

Their fear was fueled, of course, by the story of the broken-down equipment, which meant that young Soviet soldiers could be coming aboard.

The Decision

Barbi Moore had a $12 million decision to make in the next 48 hours. If she made the right one, thousands of the world's poorest of the poor would get lifesaving medicines; Mother Teresa's Missionaries of Charity in Calcutta and throughout India would get the supplies they so desperately needed for their clinics, orphanages, and hospices; 92 people from the U.S. and Europe would participate in one of the largest humanitarian airlifts in the history of India; several international companies would see the value of committing their resources to reaching out to the needy; and the year of planning by Heart to Heart International would result in the most successful project attempted by our organization.

If she made the wrong decision, the MD-11 cargo plane owned by Federal Express would be denied permission to land in Calcutta; thousands of FedEx employees who had gotten behind this airlift would never support another Heart to Heart project; Heart to Heart itself could collapse under the weight of the project's failure; the poorest and sickest residents on the planet would continue in their downward spiral; and Mother Teresa would see this as just another hollow promise of a bunch of American do-gooders.

Barbi understood the stakes.

It seemed to her, as the lone Heart to Heart representative

in one of the world's poorest cities, that maybe Heart to Heart finally faced a mountain that was too high to climb. Barbi is the director of international programs. She's been with Heart to Heart from its inception and seen all its projects through. "Until now," she thought.

The permissions alone were enough to choke the project to death. She had already met with the minister of finance, the customs commissioner, the minister of health, the drug controller, the minister of external affairs, and the police to ask permission to bring in these medicines and supplies. She did this in Calcutta, where the supplies would be distributed, and in New Delhi, the nation's capital.

She had also met with the Civil Aviation office for permission to fly into Calcutta, Airport Security for permission to have the plane and the delegation on the tarmac, the chief of police for permission to have trucks haul the supplies from site to site, the Taxation office so Heart to Heart wouldn't be charged a sales tax for bringing in these supplies, the Airport Administration office so we wouldn't be charged landing fees, and the Airport Authority for permission to take photographs while the medicines were distributed.

All offices in both cities granted her the required permissions and waivers for the project to move forward. That meant nearly 40 bureaucratic agencies had seen the project design and all of them had given the green light.

Except one.

The Customs office still hadn't waived the duty for bringing in $12 million in supplies. They wanted a lot of money—$6 million in fees that would go into the cash-starved government treasury. Waiving it would send a message to the people of India, and the officials pondered if it would be the right message. The news media would surely second-guess them. Then again, not waiving it could mean the Heart to Heart airlift could be aborted; the organization couldn't pay a 50 percent duty on life-saving materials that would be distributed by volunteers paying their own way to India.

Because of the delay from the Customs office, some of the larger hospitals that were going to receive materials from the airlift began backing out and removing their support. They no longer wanted to participate, for fear that they would get stuck with the duty for the materials. They weren't interested in bankruptcy. The wheels started falling off the wagon.

Unaware of this uncertainty, we were loading the FedEx plane in London with medicine and supplies amid much enthusiasm from FedEx employees, the U.S. Embassy, Heart to Heart volunteers, and British television. Only Barbi knew the project was in trouble.

Only Barbi knew the project was in trouble.

Then, two days before the arrival date, Barbi got a message from India's Ministry of Home Affairs. No one had asked for their permission for this airlift to occur. She turned to her business and government contacts, exasperated, and pointed to the nearly 40 clearances received.

"Can't we just ignore this one?" she asked.

She saw her associates' eyes widen.

"They are our CIA."

She let that sink in.

"How long do permissions from them typically take?"

"Three months."

It was time for a conference call. In Delhi, Barbi and her main business contact got on the line. In Calcutta were other business contacts and members of the local Rotary Club. In London were executives of Federal Express. In Kansas City were the top three Heart to Heart officers. In San Diego were members of Barbi's international operations staff. And in Memphis were the top executives of Federal Express's world headquarters.

She told everyone about the dilemma. There was no way she could predict whether these last official clearances would be granted. And there was no way she could foresee that it was soon going to get worse—Mother Teresa would fall and break her collarbone and probably not be able to meet with our delegation as she'd said. After a long silence from three continents, one gentle voice finally said, "Barbi, what do you think we should do?"

The Crisis

We had reached the crisis point in our organization. We knew that whatever decision we were about to make would change us—and not necessarily for the better. Heart to Heart, like most other nonprofit relief groups, lives by the contributions of its supporters. That's fine when there is a big project to focus on, like providing help to refugee shelters in Rwanda and earthquake shelters in Los Angeles. But maintaining a consistent level of income is difficult. There are costs to doing what we do. The few full-time staff members we have like it when they are paid consistently and on time!

In the early days of Heart to Heart, if there was a shortage of money, a board member and I would simply loan Heart to Heart the money it needed to meet its payroll and other obligations. But as Heart to Heart grew, and there was additional staff, and the projects got bigger and more expensive, the ability to personally cover our shortfalls became harder. The board member on whom I usually called for this kind of help finally said that we needed a better method, such as taking out a line of credit from a bank, rather than these personal loans. So he suggested this to our Board of Directors.

Some board members thought it was a good idea. Others were emphatic in their opposition, saying that it would show a lack of faith.

On the surface it didn't look like the kind of disagreement that was without resolution. Smart people have figured out more complex problems than this one. But it became a bigger and bigger issue, and any solution guaranteed substantial division among board members. The subject would come up at nearly every meeting, often when the time was late and we were ready to go home. It was driving a wedge between us because a vote for one side or the other signified a fundamental difference in how some board members thought Heart to Heart should be run.

If enough board members decided that they didn't like the decision we were about to make, they could resign and throw Heart to Heart into disarray—maybe even dissolve the organization. I wasn't sure that I wanted to see this dream go down the drain over a disagreement about money. Still, that was a possibility.

No one was getting angry about this. We were still brothers and sisters and respected one another. But we could all tell that we were headed for a showdown. Personally, I was leaning toward using the line of credit. It didn't seem like a lack of faith to me. It looked more like a way to even out the financial peaks and valleys. And I knew it would alleviate a great deal of stress for my development director.

I finally got tired of going back and forth on this subject and decided we needed to settle this once and for all. Were we going to borrow money or not? I called for a special board meeting and told Doug Bachtel, the board member most opposed to borrowing, to write a rationale for why we should not borrow. It was obvious to me why we should.

I knew that whatever we decided would change Heart to Heart in a dramatic way. The meeting was set to take place in the back room of a local restaurant. I told board members to come with not only open minds but also a readiness to vote. I hoped the vote would not be the beginning of the end for Heart to Heart.

I hoped the vote would not be the beginning of the end for Heart to Heart.

The Train Ride

It is one thing to have a group of people yell and gesture at you when you can understand what they are saying. It's something else entirely when you are in a different country, and you don't know a word of their language. That is the spot we found ourselves in on a train in Poland.

Four of us were carrying 10 duffel bags full of medicine destined for hospitals and clinics in the Soviet Union. The bags were with us because we had heard about supplies like this being stolen from airports and sold on the black market, and we thought it would be better if we could keep an eye on them ourselves. If companies were going to trust us by donating the medicine, we felt responsible for making sure it reached its destination. One of the ways Heart to Heart differs from other organizations is that whatever medicine or supplies we procure, we also personally distribute with volunteers.

So we first flew into Sweden with the medicine, then took a ferry across the Baltic Sea and got on a train in Hamburg, Germany, where the bags could be with us at all times. Another train took us to Berlin, and we boarded another headed for Warsaw, where the rest of the delegation volunteers planned to meet us.

But way out in the middle of Poland, our train stopped, and another pulled up next to it. We didn't know if we were to get on that train or stay put, and that was apparently the debate raging among the Polish travelers on our train. It appeared that some were telling us that we should be on the other train. I was getting the picture that there were several train stations in Warsaw, and these passengers were adamant that the other train would take us to the station we wanted. Just as many, it seemed, were telling us to stay where we were. Then they started arguing with each other. We couldn't tell exactly what they were saying, but it was obvious they felt very strongly about their opinions.

If there were several train stations, which one would the rest of our delegation choose? How would they find us if we chose different stations?

Suddenly the train we were on started moving. The shouting and arguing reached a deafening level, and we had to decide what to do. I was quiet for a moment and then yelled, "Let's go!"

We jumped off the train as it began to pick up speed, while the remaining travelers threw our 10 bags out the doors and windows and waved good-bye.

Picking up the bags, emotionally drained after the adrenaline rush, we headed for the other train. Nobody said anything, but I knew what the others were thinking: What if we chose the wrong train?

The Door of Hope

The above scenarios really happened. In each there was a moment of genuine concern—even doubt—about the outcome. The stories come from our experiences with Heart to Heart International as we have tried to find ways to help relieve suffering around the world and in our own country.

We are not so naive as to believe that whatever medicines and supplies we can provide will take care of someone's problems forever. We know that pills only last a short while, that surgical supplies eventually are used up. But as volunteers have gone with us to help distribute these supplies, something else has happened with every medical airlift we have conducted. A bond was created. Something was stirred in both those who gave and those who received.

I believe that what people have experienced in these airlifts is something all humanity craves: hope. In a world full of death, disease, and corruption, hope keeps us going.

In his book *The Soul of Politics*, Jim Wallis writes, "Hope is the door from one reality to another. Between the impossibility and possibility, there is a door, the door of hope."

In a world full of death, disease, and corruption, hope keeps us going.

In the deepest parts of every human being—in our heart and soul—is a desire for meaning and significance. My experience as a physician and as the founder of Heart to Heart International is that this meaning and significance can come from entering into the needs of other people. From serving them. That gives them—and us—hope.

"Hope is not simply a feeling or a mood or a rhetorical flourish," Wallis writes. "Hope is the very dynamic of history.

Hope is the engine of change. Hope is the energy of transformation."

This book is about how *everyone* can be a messenger of hope and, by doing so, can find meaning in their own lives. The hope you will read about is delivered in some very unconventional ways—they are extraordinary and ordinary at the same time. In fact, at Heart to Heart, we always say that we are "Ordinary people doing extraordinary things." You will see that each of us can be used to deliver hope to a seemingly hopeless world. And that each of us can move from insignificance to significance when we are messengers of hope.

Some of the people at Heart to Heart believe we are doing God's work. I believe that. So did Mother Teresa in Calcutta. She called us "pencils in the hands of God." She said that God wants to use all people as His instruments—our abilities, our experiences, our education, our time, our resources, our money, our expertise—to help the poor and suffering of the world. I believe that this is what God designed human beings to do.

The Outcomes

In the examples at the beginning of this chapter there seemed to be incredible obstacles to overcome if we were going to deliver medicine—and hope. Heart to Heart has faced too many obstacles to count—some small, some great, some impossible. But in every case something extraordinary happened, and hope was delivered.

The mounting tension on the Moscow airport tarmac eased a little when our volunteers began doing what little they could: hand-lifting boxes from the plane down to other members of our delegation, who handed them to the waiting Soviet cadets. Soon we had a human chain going from the plane to the trucks. At the rate we were going we knew it would take all day and night, but we had to start somewhere. We started with the first box within reach. Like a bucket brigade of more than 100 members, we handed out one box at a time.

We didn't know much Russian, and the cadets knew little English, so we communicated what we had to in order to get the job done. But we must have communicated something else, too, because it wasn't long before we were joking, laughing, encouraging and enjoying each other—Americans and Soviets—surmounting the language barrier.

After a couple of hours of watching us collaborate with the "enemy," the pilots loosened up and let a few more helpers on the plane. Soon the cadets and pilots were exchanging caps and other mementos—even food. By the end of the night we were talking about our families. And before we said good-bye to our Russian friends following 12 hours of intense, hard work, some of the air force crew had removed the American flag patches from their uniforms and given them to the soldiers, who proudly pinned them to their uniforms.

What had been a stalemate became a shared experience that accomplished something for the benefit of the needy.

Our volunteer delegates began the distribution to the hospitals the next day, but I needed to get back home. As we prepared the big C-5 for departure the next morning, the pilots told me, "Anytime you want to do this again, let us know. We'd love to be involved." The sick and dying had their needs met. Two pilots, and maybe just a few Russian cadets, caught a glimmer of hope.

Barbi Moore's situation in India was even more complicated. Her innocent question, "Can't we just ignore [India's CIA]?" wasn't a viable option. Actually, it didn't seem as if this airlift was an option anymore.

She had been working with a man named Tushar Jani, a Hindu with Blue Dart Express in India. He and members of the Calcutta Rotary had been helping with the government permissions. Since Tushar was a well-respected businessman in India, he arranged meetings with the Ministry of Customs, the Ministry of Finance, and the Ministry of Home Affairs on one day's notice. He and Barbi then flew from Calcutta to New Delhi for the emergency meetings. They carried with them letters from the U.S. Consulate in Calcutta and from the U.S. ambassador to India at the time, Frank Wisner, asking the Indian government to expedite help for this airlift.

Home Affairs and Finance signed the permissions without

incident. Customs was still not convinced. Barbi and Tushar told the minister that the airlift involved Mother Teresa, good-will between India and the U.S., and that members of the minister's office were invited to be on the tarmac of the airport when the plane arrived.

During this discussion the minister removed a rubber stamp and ink pad from his desk and ceremoniously thumped our written request. Barely breaking the flow of the conversation, Tushar turned to Barbi and said softly, "He just waived the whole thing," and then returned to the ongoing discussion.

Barbi tried to continue participating, but her tears streamed nonstop. "God has used you, Tushar," she kept repeating.

The airlift was on.

To resolve our board meeting dilemma, we desperately needed that door of transformation that Jim Wallis describes. Any of you who have been on boards involving businesses, churches, or any other kind of organization can understand the seriousness of our situation. We knew it was a turning point for us. But what if we took the wrong turn? As the day of the special meeting approached, we knew that we needed to take some kind of action.

We knew it was a turning point for us. But what if we took the wrong turn?

We needed that door to take us from one reality to another.

A few days before our showdown meeting, I got a call from a friend who said he had met someone recently and thought I should meet him too. My friend said that this person was interested in knowing more about Heart to Heart. The man was a surgeon and also the grandson of J. Hudson Taylor.

I was instantly intrigued, remembering that J. Hudson Taylor was one of the pioneer missionaries to China during the latter part of the 19th century, and people around the world respected him for his work. I really wanted to meet this grandson because I was exploring the idea of having Heart to Heart conduct an airlift to China. But my schedule was extremely tight, so I told my friend that the only time I had was during this special board meeting, and that Dr. Taylor was welcome to meet us at the restaurant. It wasn't ideal, but it was the best I could do.

I was really looking forward to this board meeting because we had discussed this topic a dozen times and wanted to reach a consensus. I explained and even apologized to the board that I had invited a guest, but suggested we could proceed as if he knew everything about us.

I introduced our guest as a doctor who was interested in our work, and we began.

Doug Bachtel, the board member most vehement in his opposition to borrowing money, said he wanted to read a statement that was in a devotional book he had been using recently. The quote was "God's work, done in God's way, will never lack God's supply."

Doug once again articulated his belief that if this was God's work, then we should expect Him to provide for us, and that we shouldn't borrow the money. Then he described the man who made the above statement as a missionary who was famous for his great faith. He believed that you should not even ask someone to support you, nor that you should take an offering. He believed that you should simply pray, letting God know your needs, and then wait for the answer. If you did not get the money you wanted, then you should just do without, this missionary said.

Doug was saying the same thing—that we should do what we could with the resources we had, and that God would bring us the resources at the time we needed them.

"Who was that missionary?" asked another board member.

"His name is J. Hudson Taylor, a missionary to China a long time ago," Doug said.

I couldn't believe my ears. Never in any meeting that I'd attended, let alone a Heart to Heart meeting, had J. Hudson Taylor been quoted.

I looked suspiciously at Doug, and then at our visitor.

"Have you two ever met?" I asked them both.

Both men shook their heads.

"You aren't going to believe this," I said. "The Dr. Taylor right here is the grandson of J. Hudson Taylor."

Everyone got very quiet.

"Did your grandfather really say that?" I asked our visitor.

"It is his most famous statement," Dr. Taylor said.

We voted and decided not to borrow any money.

Regarding our great Polish train adventure, we made the right choice. Of all the stations the waiting volunteers could have chosen, the train we hopped on took us to the one they had guessed.

The next obstacle was getting through the border checkpoint from Poland into Russia. These border checkpoints going from one Eastern European country to another were as intimidating as you can imagine during the days of the Soviet Union.

We watched for a while, surrounded by barbed wire, guns, and snow.

When we reached the end of the line in Poland, Russian soldiers in heavy hats, coats, and armaments gruffly ordered us off. We didn't speak Russian and probably weren't given a reason anyway, but soon after we got off, we understood.

Engine by engine, car by car, the train needed hoisting into the air so the wheels could be removed and replaced. They needed a new set to accommodate Russian tracks, which were a different width than Poland's. Why? It was a defensive move by Russia years ago to avoid invasion by way of trains. It was a cold, wintry Wednesday night. The wheel replacement procedure takes hours. We watched for a while, surrounded by barbed wire, guns, and snow. We hadn't anticipated this stop.

Jim Kerr, one of our volunteers, turned to me, as if he had just come from a Laurel and Hardy movie, and said, "Well, this is another fine mess you've gotten us into, Gary!"

With that, we headed off into the little Russian town. We thought some exploring might kill some time and keep us warmer than standing around the unheated train station.

An intriguing-looking building caught our eyes. It was a Russian Orthodox church, complete with the onion-shaped tower. It needed a lot of repair. The outside fence was broken and rusting. Windows were boarded up. It hadn't been painted in decades. Pieces of the eaves and roof moved with the bitter, cold wind.

But what got our attention was that it looked like a light was on inside. We moved closer, feeling more brave because of each other, and finally got next to the building so we could see through a space in the boards. We thought we heard something going on in there.

We were all startled when the giant oak door creaked open next to us, and a thin Russian man stepped out. We greeted him, and he motioned us in.

This former house of God had been transformed into a military tank repair facility for the central government. It was filled with junk—boxes, truck parts, grease, and ice-cold dust. The Russian dictator Vladimir Lenin declared in 1917 that there would be no more centers of worship. The facilities after the Revolution would serve the government.

Then we remembered the light. Where was it coming from? We looked around until we found it—high above us in the belfry of the tall tower. Near the light, collected on makeshift scaffolding, was a choir. Practicing.

They stopped when they saw us. We looked up and sheepishly called out a Russian greeting that no doubt sounded like four Americans trying to sound Russian. They called down their own greeting and then gave us a gift that was more valuable than they'll ever know. They sang us a hymn. A cappella. In beautiful harmony.

The four of us applauded, waved, and thanked them. We understood that the light was a promise that God was indeed in Russia. He had not been extinguished during the darkness of this country's brutal religious oppression. The hymn was an affirmation that His people were alive, believing, and full of hope.

So were we, in a fresh way. The cathedral that had been used for decades as a tank repair shop had been briefly restored to its original intent. We knew then that it was only a matter of time before the Russian people would again be allowed to worship the God of life. We knew that Communism could not prevail over what we had just witnessed.

This wasn't an evil empire. This country had a light. It had a hope.

Hope is the engine of change, Wallis said. "Hope is believing in spite of the evidence and watching the evidence change."

I think that hope is more than just *believing* in spite of the evidence. It is taking action. The evidence changed on the tarmac in Moscow, in the Customs office in New Delhi, at that restaurant conference room in Kansas City, and in the decaying cathedral in Russia as we took action. The resulting hope transformed the situations, hearts, and souls of those involved. Activity of God. Ordinary people serving one another.

2

"Semper Fi, Bob"

Bob Lewis is a logistics guy. He looks at a situation, decides whether it is worth pursuing, develops a tactical plan to resolve it, procures the resources to achieve success, and carries out the mission. Sound like a kind of person you've heard about?

You got it. He's Marine Corps through and through.

As a special operations officer, he served two tours in Vietnam and claims there is still a price on his head in that country. He made colonel there. He's retired now, but while a retired marine may not be officially on active duty, he is always active in some way. Once a marine always a marine, retired or not.

So when Mike Meyers told Bob about another mission to Vietnam, Bob perked up. And thought logistics.

Mike thought about Bob after attending one of our Heart to Heart meetings, where we talked about conducting a medical airlift to Vietnam during the 20th anniversary of the end of the war. Mike, also a Vietnam war veteran, said he knew someone who could speak and write Vietnamese fluently. He had met Bob at the school where Mike's son attended, where Bob was the dean of admissions.

Mike knew that Bob's missions were extremely complicated; his experiences would be a valuable resource for our airlift.

At first Bob wasn't interested. He said he had seen other groups involving veterans go back there, and no matter how pure their intentions were at the beginning, they were co-opted by someone else's political agenda.

But Mike's approach was different. He was talking about a

group of volunteers going there, strictly for humanitarian reasons. It was people who wanted to help relieve the suffering that still existed after the war.

So Colonel Bob came to a few meetings where I explained that we had millions of dollars in medicine and medical supplies that we wanted to distribute there. And, ever the marine, he saw logistical problems with our mission.

"I saw weaknesses in their ability to deal with the diplomatic issues of the day," Bob said later. "They needed a tactical plan that would not be so open to criticism from veterans groups too."

Still, Bob kept an open mind because, as he said, "I thought this mission was the right thing to do."

He saw, as I did, that the biggest problem with our idea was that there was no inexpensive way to transport the supplies to Vietnam. On our previous airlifts to Russia, Armenia, the Ukraine, and elsewhere, we had the support of the U.S. State Department. They had provided cargo planes and the pilots. They were reluctant to get involved in such a politically charged project as Vietnam. And there was no way Heart to Heart could even dream of paying for the shipping of these medicines.

Then Bob spoke up at one of our meetings.

"I know a guy who has airplanes," he said.

We were listening. "Who?" I asked.

"His name is Fred Smith. He's at Federal Express."

I was well aware of Fred Smith. He is the chief executive officer for the world's leading package transportation company.

And I was also aware that Fred Smith wasn't interested in a project conducted by Heart to Heart. We had already asked and had a "Sorry, we can't help you at this time" letter in a file bulging with similar letters.

It's not that FedEx didn't have a heart. The company historically had worked with the Red Cross but wasn't adding members to their list of relief organizations. I couldn't get to first base with those guys.

But I underestimated the colonel.

"Freddy was in my platoon when I was a marine lieutenant in Quantico, Virginia," Bob said. "I'll ask him."

Freddy? Frankly, I didn't think Bob would have any more success than I had. They hadn't spoken to each other since the Quantico days, which were before they both served in Vietnam. Nearly 25 years. But I encouraged him to do whatever he could.

He wrote a letter to "Freddy" Smith, excerpted here:

I have a proposal for you that may be of commercial benefit as well as personally rewarding to an old marine company commander. I'm donating my time to an organization called Heart to Heart International, that delivers medicines to stricken areas of the world. . . .

We are going [to Vietnam] in May, and you should be with us. It would be a chance to visit the country, not the war. One reason that I support Heart to Heart is that rather than sending medicine—they take it. The difference is the same as the difference in "commitment" to breakfast of a chicken and of a pig. We, like the pig, are *really* committed. . . .

[T]he greatest reward will be actually delivering medicines, not to the government, not to some nameless bureaucrats, but right to the doctors in the hospitals. . . .

I suspect everyone would like to see your FedEx tail number arrive in Da Nang. You would bring special credentials to the mission, both as a marine and businessman of equal distinction. Few of us can do that. If we are ever to really treat Vietnam as a country, not a war, the impetus will have to come from men like you. . . .

Semper Fidelis,

Bob Lewis, Col. USMC (ret.), late of Co. C

Once I read this very simple appeal, I felt even less encouraged. I didn't think it was very well stated. In fact, I commented to some of the staff that there was no way Fred Smith would ever respond to a letter like that. The letter was too long; Colonel Bob rambled on about things that I thought had little to do with the airlift. But we proceeded with our plan to carry the project forward.

One week later, at about 8:30 P.M., Colonel Bob got a telephone call from Fred Smith.

They talked for about five minutes, Bob said. Mr. Smith just had one question: Did Bob really think this was the right thing to do?

Fred Smith didn't ask about the cost or the business benefit to Federal Express. He only wanted to know if it was right.

Bob told him that enough time had passed, and that this was as good a way as any to change the way our countries dealt with each other. Bob said that a non-governmental agency like this could do far more than the governments could.

But what was most convincing to Smith was Bob's overriding mission.

Fred Smith didn't ask about the cost or the business benefit to Federal Express. He only wanted to know if it was right.

"The people of Vietnam are in desperate shape since the war," he told Smith. "It is not my desire to see them continue suffering."

"Tell me what you need," Smith said.

Soon Federal Express told its employees and the public that now there were *two* groups where the company would concentrate its charitable efforts: the Red Cross and Heart to Heart.

Fred Smith got us the airplane and pilots—two men who had previously bombed the very city where we were to land. Only this time we were coming to Hanoi and Ho Chi Minh City (formerly Saigon) to heal wounds, not create them.

Mike's simple declaration, "I know a guy who speaks Vietnamese," and Bob's statement, "I know a guy who has airplanes," taught me a valuable lesson: Everyone has a network. Everyone has a sphere of influence in which he or she lives and interacts—even if the sphere existed 25 years before, as it did with Col. Bob Lewis and Fred Smith. And that network can be used to meet the needs of others, to transform us into instruments of hope.

Three Stuffed Animals

One of the most haunting sights I have ever seen was in an orphanage in Calcutta, where I was looking into places that could use medical supplies from a future airlift.

This orphanage stopped me in my tracks.

The medical needs of the children were as severe as any other major city's orphanage. Some were there to die. Some were perfectly healthy but just didn't have anywhere else to go. It housed 500 children—from babies to school-age—and clearly qualified as a recipient of our donated supplies and medicine.

But what really caught my eye was a glass case, with a large lock, in the middle of the orphanage. The sisters took children to the case and let them look in. The children put their noses against the case, put their hands against it, pointed to the inside, oohing and ahhing.

I looked over the tops of their heads to see what could possibly be so fascinating. Was there a pet in there? Some kind of museum display?

What really caught my eye was a glass case, with a large lock, in the middle of the orphanage.

What I saw broke my heart. There were three stuffed animals in that case. They were locked inside because there were only three, for 500 children. Dividing them equally would mean each child would get a little tuft of worn, dirty polyester fur. So in order for all of the children to just *see* the animals, they remained out of touch, protected by a glass.

Federal Express was again participating in this airlift, and they sent a few employees after my initial visit to also inspect some sites. One of those employees was bothered by the very thing that bothered me. Three stuffed animals for 500 kids.

He was so moved that, when he returned to his London office, he told his fellow employees what he saw, and then established a collection point for donated stuffed animals that would go back to Calcutta with the medical airlift. When the supplies landed in Calcutta a few months later, we had 10,000 stuffed animals to give away.

Every child in that orphanage got to choose one to keep as his or her own, as did all the children we encountered on that trip. The toys were no longer so scarce that they were museum pieces. There were plenty for everyone.

Who wants to live forever?

FedEx did something else that had a dramatic impact on the success of the project. After viewing the thousands of sick and dying and abandoned in Calcutta during a visit before the airlift, a member of a FedEx video crew thought about a song that would be a perfect sound track for a videotaped report on what we were doing. It was a song by Freddy Mercury, the lead singer for the British rock band Queen, called "Who Wants to Live Forever?"

Mercury had died of an AIDS-related illness since that song was recorded. It was a haunting, poignant song that reflected the hopelessness we saw throughout Calcutta.

A member of the video crew called Queen's management group in London, asked for permission to use the lyrics, and told them about the video and the airlift. The management staff sounded very interested, and then they asked, "Will you be getting supplies to any AIDS facilities there?"

The crew member said that we were, and they replied, "Maybe we could give some money too."

The band had established the Mercury Phoenix Trust, named for their lead singer, to support efforts that helped AIDS victims.

They gave us a generous gift and asked if some of the band members could volunteer on the airlift.

I Know Someone Who . . .

One of the most effective means we have for accomplishing our goal of meeting needs of others is someone beginning a sentence with, "I know someone who . . ."

Through that approach we have gotten airplanes, medicines, and stuffed animals.

I remember sitting in church one Sunday, soon after we had gotten the go-ahead from the U.S. State Department to provide a medical airlift to Russia. We had a C-5 cargo plane and had procured enough medicine and supplies to fill it. But as I sat with my family, listening to the choir, it dawned on me that there was something else we needed for this airlift to occur. We needed a way to get the supplies on and off the plane. How were we going to do that?

There was no way to do it by hand. There were about 160 pallets, with 40 heavy boxes on each. Altogether they filled a giant warehouse. But they needed to fill a giant plane. The prospect of having to hand-carry each box made the airlift seem impossible.

Seated right in front of me in church was Lonnie Houk, who I knew worked in some capacity in the military.

After church I told him what Heart to Heart was trying to do, and asked if he knew where I could get some advice.

"I know a commander in the military who I think could help you," he said. "Let me see what I can do."

Later he said, "I know how to get this done."

Lonnie and the commander helped us in a way I never dreamed possible. They had a military unit do their annual summer two-week training session with us. Thanks to Lonnie, we had soldiers officially assigned to our airlift. They helped us sort, pack, inventory, and load the plane!

Because of the tremendous support the military has given Heart to Heart, I have become a member of an Army Reserve MASH hospital. I've met many more dedicated military leaders who have wanted to get their soldiers involved in spreading hope throughout the world. Another result of networking.

It is important to remember, though, what is behind a network. Living our lives in a way that brings hope to a hurting world isn't just a matter of how well connected we are. It must be grounded in our life's purpose. Why are we on this earth? What is our motivation for what we do? Will we make a difference?

Being well connected might help us achieve material success, but it won't satisfy our deep hunger for meaning. Using that network to help someone is a response to the call deep within us.

Just Pray

The first time I met Mother Teresa, Heart to Heart had not yet been born. I knew that I was being led into some kind of new direction for service, so I visited her to learn more about how her missions were organized and how she supported them.

I was particularly interested in the way she financed her organization. I knew that I had never received a direct mail

> *Being well connected might help us achieve material success, but it won't satisfy our deep hunger for meaning.*

letter from her asking for money. I had never been asked to sponsor one of the orphans in Calcutta. How did she do it? I decided to ask her so that I could possibly utilize her methods.

"Mother Teresa, what kind of development office do you have?" I asked.

She looked at me with a very perplexed face.

"What do you mean?" she said.

"How is your fund-raising organized, and who runs it for you?"

She raised her eyebrows, then shrugged her shoulders.

"We pray," she said.

Dumb me. Why hadn't I thought of that? But then, surely there must be more to it, I reasoned. So I asked once more: "How do you raise your support? Who runs the development office?"

"We just pray."

About three years later I visited her again, this time after Heart to Heart was organized and conducting airlifts. I wanted to get her approval for Heart to Heart to undertake an airlift in Calcutta.

"Mother Teresa, Heart to Heart would like to bring medicines and medical supplies to help you in your work," I said.

"That would be wonderful," she said. "We really need them. In fact, someone brought us medicines just this morning."

She pointed to a small, beat-up box in the corner.

"See—isn't this wonderful?" she said.

I looked. It was an odd assortment of medicines, mostly samples, many of them outdated. What good would one little box of medicines do in a country with such great need?

"Mother, we want to bring you a whole planeload of medicines," I said.

Remembering that I had brought along some photos of one of our airlifts, I pulled them out. They showed 40 pallets, each stacked 12 feet high, on the tarmac of an airport next to a C-5 cargo plane.

Mother Teresa's eyes widened bigger than I had ever seen them.

Mother Teresa's eyes widened bigger than I had ever seen them.

"Where did you get all that medicine?"

I remembered our conversation several years back, when I was asking her a similar question—How do you do it? Now our roles were reversed. Mother Teresa was asking me—How do you do it? Smiling, I answered, "Easy! We just pray!"

Actually, we do more than pray. On every airlift, we face obstacles like those mentioned in chapter 1. We pray and proceed, and extraordinary events transpire. Each involves people using their networks of influence to help someone in need. *Everyone* has a network.

In Spite of the Evidence

I have discovered something about networks; they almost never emerge when we are standing still. Instead, they appear after we set our plan in motion and act as if it is going to succeed. We act in spite of the evidence. Then we watch the evidence change.

Patrick Allen, an educator in San Diego, tells of attending the funeral of a family friend named J. L. Harris, who was a former county road commissioner in Tennessee. As different people paid tribute to Harris, one person told about the time during the depression when Harris was driving the back roads of the county, looking for places that needed repair.

He saw a farmer plowing his field along the road, and he pulled the car over to watch. Finally he got out of his car and approached the farmer.

"I don't know why, but I feel that I should give you this money."

Harris handed the farmer $18. The farmer nearly fell over from surprise.

"When I got up this morning, I knew I didn't have enough money to buy seeds for planting," the farmer told Harris. The money from Harris would pay for enough seeds for the man's entire crop.

What struck Patrick Allen as amazing is not that Harris gave the money to the farmer. People do extraordinary things for no tangible reason all the time, he said.

"What floored me was that the farmer was out there plowing anyway, knowing that he didn't have anything to put into the ground once he plowed it," Allen said.

Now *that*'s vision, faith—and hope! But it also describes the network that we can't always see. The farmer had gotten up that morning, saw what he didn't have, and felt that God told him to go ahead as if he knew how it would all turn out. So he plowed. He believed in spite of the evidence. If he hadn't, J. L. Harris would have never seen him. But he did, and the evidence changed.

Can you imagine Noah's initial reluctance when God instructed him to build an ark?

"Hmmm. It hasn't rained much lately. The almanac calls for more dry weather. No floods in the last few hundred years. Yup. Better get the lumber."

If we waited for the evidence to change before we acted, we'd never get out of our chairs in our search for meaning.

Consider Mary, when she was told that she would bear the Son of God.

"Not a problem. It's not the way I learned about such things in school. I've never even had a boyfriend until Joseph, and he has kept his distance. Sure. Boil the water."

Noah started swinging the hammer. Mary started spreading the news. And the evidence changed.

Will Rogers said, "Even if you're on the right track, you'll get run over if you just sit there."

If we had waited for the evidence to change, we would have never gone to Vietnam. There were too many obstacles. The United States government had an economic embargo on that country that kept people in the U.S. from attempting any kind of interaction. And yet we knew that people there were suffering. Some hospitals hadn't been repaired since we bombed them 20 years ago. There weren't enough doctors. Shortages of medicines allowed diseases easily controlled in this country to spread unchecked. It is one of the few countries where leprosy still rages.

If we had waited for the evidence to change, we would have never gone to Vietnam.

We couldn't get much cooperation in this country for the project at first. The Vietnamese were still considered the enemy. There was still some embarrassment over what happened there in the '60s and '70s. And hostility. But the people of Vietnam have fought wars throughout their country's existence—dozens of wars over hundreds of years. Now they were asking their former enemy for help. The war was over, they said.

It isn't as easy for Americans to get past that war. We had difficulty generating interest in providing the Vietnamese with medicine and hope. Our biggest obstacle was getting the medicines over there. An American aircraft had not flown into that country since the evacuation of (then) Saigon in 1975. No one seemed ready to commit to being the first in the postwar period. Still, we proceeded.

And Mike Meyers said, "I know someone who speaks Vietnamese."

And Col. Bob Lewis said, "I know a guy who has airplanes."

And Fred Smith said, "Tell me what you need."

Soon the evidence changed.

Soon we were there. Soon CNN followed us everywhere we went. Soon we got a letter from Christopher "Kit" Bond, U.S. senator from Missouri who accompanied us on the airlift: "Heart to Heart's airlift of medicines and supplies was one of the most exciting projects on which I have had the pleasure to work," he wrote.

And soon we got this letter from Le Van Bang, Vietnam's ambassador to the United States: "Our country believes that the April airlift of $7 million in medicines was instrumental in influencing the president of your country to normalize relations with our country."

Everyone has a network. You usually find it when you're in motion. And you usually find meaning in your life when you use that network to help someone. Try an experiment: Watch your sense of purpose grow when you see a need and you begin your next sentence with, "I know someone who . . ."

3

JESUS WAS
A BUSBOY

I COULD TELL HE WAS GETTING FRUSTRATED. HE couldn't quite get the words out, but he kept trying and trying. He was speaking from his wheelchair, and I was leaning toward him, but I still couldn't get it. I turned to his wife.

"Cyndi, what's he saying?" I asked.

I was at the home of my good friends Steve and Cyndi Lamb, and we were talking about things we were doing at Heart to Heart and all of the places we had been.

Steve and Cyndi have been close to my wife and me for years. Steve was one of the brightest, most creative people I knew. He was confined to a wheelchair after a drunk driver hit him head-on as he was driving to church one Sunday morning. We didn't know if he would survive the accident. His spinal cord didn't, but his incredible brain and spirit did. Still, he had a great deal of trouble speaking. I could tell that he was thinking something profound, but he couldn't get the words out of his mouth.

It was coming out in short phrases.

He said something like, "Think small," several times, and then he kept trying to say something else that, no matter how hard I tried, eluded me. That's when I asked Cyndi for help.

"I think he's saying, 'Jesus was a busboy,'" she said.

I looked at Steve, unsure that she was right; and even if she was, what did that statement mean?

Then he said it again—slowly, haltingly, awkwardly. I felt embarrassed for him that he wanted to say something so badly but was having so much difficulty.

So I asked him, "Jesus was a busboy? That's what you're trying to say?"

He nodded emphatically. He had me look up a story in the Bible where Jesus was at a wedding.

"His first miracle," Steve said, through Cyndi.

In the story the people at the wedding ran out of wine, and Jesus' mother told Him that they needed more to drink.

Steve said that Mary spoke to Jesus the same way we would speak to a guy with a tray walking through the restaurant: "Can we have more to drink, here?" The first thing Jesus did, Steve said, was turn six jars of water into wine, and everyone had plenty of quality beverage.

Now *I* was the one getting frustrated. It had taken a long time to get all of this said, but still I didn't understand.

Cyndi explained Steve's point. When he had his car accident, the people who helped them the most were those who did the small things. People who took his kids to Little League practice. People who gave his wife gasoline credit cards so she didn't have to worry about that detail while taking care of three kids and a quadriplegic husband. People who did grocery shopping and baby-sitting. People who mowed the lawn.

Steve understood that you don't have to go to Russia to perform miracles. You can probably just go as far as your next-door neighbor.

"Think small," he kept saying.

He was right, of course.

Thinking small is the way Heart to Heart began.

Beginnings

Thinking small is the way Heart to Heart began. Nobody sat around a conference room table and said, "How can we relieve the suffering of major disaster victims, using high-quality pharmaceuticals and supplies donated to us by the largest manufacturers in the world?"

That was the farthest thing from my mind.

When I decided to become a doctor, I wanted, from the very

beginning, to volunteer some of my time to help the poor and needy of the world. I didn't know if that meant I would be in third world countries or the inner cities of the U.S. After I opened my private practice, I gave several weeks a year to working in various mission hospitals around the world. As I mentioned in the Prologue, I had just returned from working in refugee camps in Vietnam and Cambodia one year when I walked into my local Rotary Club after the meeting had begun.

"Glad to see you, Dr. Morsch," the man at the podium said. "Our speaker for today has not arrived—would you be so kind as to come up and tell about your latest medical mission trip?"

So I did. I described the trip and told them I thought it was important to realize how much we have in this country, and how a simple act of sharing can break down walls of ignorance, fear, and stereotypes. Trips like this were hard work, I said, but the reward of seeing the breadth of the human family made it all worthwhile.

I told the group that, in my view, we had an obligation to give from our excess to those who had nothing.

Then, without thinking, I suggested that this Rotary Club should take on a project somewhere in the world.

The group began brainstorming. Over the next few weeks we found out about a run-down YWCA in Belize (the former British Honduras), near Mexico. In 1989 a group of Rotarians went there for a week. We did some construction work, roofing, a lot of painting and patching, and within a week the YWCA looked pretty good. We had a great time interacting with the people of that city. We felt good about how we had spent our time and resources.

More important, though, we felt as if we had done something that had significance. We helped someone. We didn't change the world; that wasn't our goal. But some people in Belize now have a usable facility that they didn't have before. And we have friends that we didn't have before.

Through that experience, both the group that went to Mexico and the group that stayed behind in support began to catch the vision of what it means for human beings to help one another. We immediately started raising money for a trip the following year. That time we went to St. Croix in the Virgin Islands to help rebuild some buildings that had blown down during Hurricane Hugo.

Through these trips, our monthly meetings took on a completely different tone. We had a purpose.

Remembering Chernobyl

In 1991 one of our members had a *big* idea. The five-year anniversary of the Chernobyl nuclear disaster was coming up, and this member, Dan Ostegaard, was with the American Academy of Family Practice. He had heard that health care in that part of the world was inadequate to deal with the physical problems resulting from the release of so much radiation. People were still in desperate shape from the fallout.

This kind of concern for others had been a way of life for Dan for a long time. His parents had been missionaries in India, and he grew up on a Navajo reservation while his parents worked in ministry there. In addition to being a family practice doctor and an administrator for the Academy, he was also a volunteer with World Vision, another relief agency.

For a trip to the Chernobyl area, we thought, providing medicine would be more useful than repairing buildings.

Then Dan's idea got even bigger: What if, somehow, we could have an impact on how health care is provided in that region?

The Soviet medical system was based on specialization. Certain doctors and hospitals deal only with burns, others with orthopedics, others with cancer, others with other specific diseases. The concept of family practice—one primary physician for most of a person's medical needs—was foreign. And in light of how many people were still suffering in that area, that kind of specialization was extremely inefficient.

But having a broad-range impact on health care would take time, Dan knew. First, he had to think small.

We all knew that delivering drugs to the region was a small gesture, and that it would only be a matter of time before the drugs would run out. But Dan was thinking about the future too. He thought starting small like this could lead to something else.

Even if it didn't, though, and the relief we brought was only temporary, "It was better than not doing anything," he said.

"Delivering medicine is a transient activity," he said. "But you need to do the transient in order to do the enduring."

We made the trip. We've been back several times. The idea of family practice is becoming an option.

Dan's notion of the transient leading to the enduring was evident during one of his subsequent trips to the area—this time in the Ukraine. A Russian doctor worked as his translator and guide throughout one of our trips there. He introduced Dan to other doctors and helped ensure that the medicines we had brought actually reached their destinations.

> " Delivering medicine is a transient activity," he said. "But you need to do the transient in order to do the enduring."

The day Dan was to leave the Ukraine and take an 18-hour train trip to Kyiv (formerly Kiev), where hospitals there also needed supplies, he said that his doctor/translator made an impression on him. Some of the doctors we encounter on these trips show a tremendous amount of compassion for their people, even though their facilities and supplies are so few. Other doctors aren't so motivated because they know they will get their small salary whether they work or not.

This doctor sincerely wanted to help despite the shortages. As Dan got ready to leave, he reached in a box and gave the doctor a stethoscope. Dan said the doctor gasped—in his whole professional life he would have never had his own stethoscope.

Dan gave him a tool that was not consumable the way a pill is. This was enduring. The contact, the respect, the mutual desire to help the needy—all shown in the symbol of a stetho-

scope—is enduring. But it came after the transient task of bringing medicine and supplies. As I have said many times in regard
to Heart to Heart and to being instruments in the hands of God,
this effort isn't about pills—it's about people.

More than Comfort

What Steve Lamb and Dan Ostegaard have realized is the
same conclusion Mother Teresa came to in 1952 when she opened
the Home for Dying Destitutes. She had already been in a convent in India since 1929, but in 1946, on a train headed for a spiritual retreat center, she sensed God's calling to follow Him even
more deeply. By 1948 she had moved out of her convent and,
with five rupees, started a school in the poorest of the poor
neighborhoods of Calcutta. The school had five children, and she
began by teaching them the alphabet. Then personal hygiene.

Gradually the work grew as ladies from Calcutta who used
to be teachers came to help. The school survived and expanded
with donations because, from the very first, she did not ask for
money.

Doctors and nurses also came to the school on a volunteer
basis. And that is when she decided to open a Home for Dying
Destitutes—a place for people on the streets who have been
abandoned and left for dead.

"The first woman I saw, I myself picked up from the
street," Mother Teresa told Malcolm Muggeridge. "She had
been half eaten by the rats and ants. I took her to a hospital, but
they could not do anything for her. They only took her in because I refused to move until they accepted her."

From there Mother Teresa went to city officials and asked
them to give her a place where she could bring other dying people she had seen on the streets.

I have seen Mother Teresa in action. I have seen her deal
with government officials both in India and the United States.
She was a very insistent woman. Because she so strongly believed she was doing what God told her to do, she was fearless.

The government gave Mother Teresa a building only two
blocks away from the temple dedicated to Kali, the Hindu god-
dess of wrath and destruction. Calcutta is the center of Kali

worship. Within 24 hours after the government granted her request, Mother Teresa had people in the building—the dying and
destitute.

In a few years more than 20,000 people had spent their last
days in the care of Mother Teresa
and the Missionaries of Charity. At
first other sisters would find these
people in the streets and bring
them to the building, as Mother
Teresa did for the first woman. But
as the work became known, residents of Calcutta would call the
city ambulance to pick up people
from the street. The only condition
Mother Teresa put on accepting
someone was that the person had
nowhere else to go—this home
would be the last refuge.

Within 24 hours after the government granted her request, Mother Teresa had people in the building— the dying and destitute.

Mother Teresa's ministry began when she responded to one
person she saw on the street. She
was thinking small.

Why would she reach out to a
dying woman she didn't even
know? Because the worst human disease, she says, is to be un-
wanted.

"We want them to know human and divine love," she said.
"We want to make them feel that they are wanted; we want
them to know that there are people who really love them, who
really want them, at least for the few hours that they have to
live. That they, too, may know that they are the children of God,
and that they are not forgotten."

Mother Teresa added one more item in the interview with
Malcolm Muggeridge, an item that seemed subtle but has be-
come part of the underpinning of why Heart to Heart exists.
"There are young lives ready to give themselves in their ser-
vice," she said. You see, most of the people who join the work in
Calcutta are educated and from middle-class to upper-class

homes. Likewise, people who volunteer to go with us on our airlifts often have comfortable lives. But they know that life is more than comfort.

One man from Australia gave Mother Teresa a large donation, but then, after giving the donation, he said, "Money is something outside of me, but I want to give something of me." Now he comes regularly to the Home for Dying Destitutes, where he shaves the men and visits with them.

"I just ask them to come and love the people, to give their hands to serve them, and their hearts to love them," Mother Teresa said. "When they come in touch with them, then their first impulse is to do something for them."

Something as small as giving someone a shave.

If you are like most people I talk with, though, you're asking the same question Muggeridge asked Mother Teresa. In the grand scheme of things, what have you really accomplished if you help one person be comfortable for a few days? Most people, Muggeridge said, consider their meager efforts "a fleabite" and see that they haven't permanently changed anything. People still starve, people still get diseases, people still die. Misery abounds whether or not you do anything. It's all so, so, *small*.

Something as small as giving someone a shave.

In other words, does *any* good come from thinking small?

Listen to Mother Teresa: "I do not agree with the big way of doing things. What matters is an individual. To get to love the person, we must come in close contact with him. If we wait till we get the numbers, then we will be lost in the numbers.

"I never look at crowds; I look at people. If I thought about crowds, I would never start anything. I believe in person to person."

So, taking Steve Lamb's kids to Little League, giving Dan Ostegaard's translator a stethoscope, taking medicine to radiation victims in Russia, providing a bed to a dying person—in the grand scheme of things, does it matter?

If you think small, it does.

"If we didn't have our schools in the slums," Mother Teresa said, "they are nothing, they are just little primary schools where we teach the children to love the school and to be clean and so on—if we didn't have these little schools, those children, those thousands of children, would be left in the streets. So we have to choose either to take them and give them just a little, or leave them in the street.

"It is the same thing for our home for the dying and our home for the children. If we didn't have that home, those people we have picked up, they would have died in the street. I think it was worthwhile having that home even for those few people to die beautifully, with God and in peace."

There is a sign in the Home for Dying Destitutes that defines her actions: Do Small Things with Great Love. It hangs in the laundry/dishwashing/garbage area, where small things occur day and night.

> *There is a sign in the Home for Dying Destitutes that defines her actions: Do Small Things with Great Love.*

Small Things with Great Love

In his book *Letters to a Young Doctor*, Richard Selzer tells of going to the downtown public library on Wednesdays, his day off, and sitting in the main reading room to look at newspapers and magazines from around the world. Several elderly people in that room were regulars, enjoying the fringe benefits of a facility like that: a warm, dry building with working toilets and a vending machine that had hot broth or coffee.

Selzer noticed that on one particular day, a gentleman seemed to have a great deal of trouble walking. Each step was a fresh onslaught of pain.

"His lower lip was caught between his teeth," Selzer wrote.

"His forehead had been cut and stitched into lines of endurance. He was hissing."

Selzer asked the man what was wrong.

"The toes."

"What's wrong with the toes?"

"The toenails is too long. I can't get at 'em. I'm walkin' on 'em."

Selzer left the library and went to his office to retrieve his toenail clippers. When he returned, he took the man aside and began working on the toenails. It took him an hour to do each big toe. The following week he did the toes of another regular. Then another.

"I never go to the library on Wednesday afternoon without my nail clippers in my briefcase," he wrote. "You just never know."

Selzer didn't solve one of the great health care problems in this country, or even in that town. Clipping toenails doesn't cure heart disease or cancer. But Richard Selzer isn't called to do great things, and neither are you. Our job is to do small things. With great love.

Selzer's Wednesdays took on new meaning because, in a small way, he was helping someone. Even though he helps people as part of his profession on the other days of the week, his days off now have more significance. It's how we're meant to live.

When we went on our first trip to Belize, that was as big as we ever dreamed our Rotary project would get. We treated it as if it were the right thing at the time, much as Mother Teresa did when she started teaching the alphabet to five children who lived on the streets of Calcutta. She wasn't concerned with what this would grow into. She was only concerned with what God had put in her life that day. That's how we looked at refurbishing that YWCA.

"*This* is the day the LORD has made," the psalmist wrote (118:24, NIV, emphasis added). Think today. Think small.

Larger than Life

When Jesus was coming to the end of His time on earth, He

wanted to get across His call to discipleship in one last poignant way. I can think of lots of things He could have done, can't you? The recording secretary could have given a rundown of all the miracles, starting with the unusual circumstances around His birth: Gabriel's visit to Mary, Bethlehem, angels singing to shepherds, wise men following a star, and so on. Then the Baptism, the water into wine thing, the raising of Lazarus, the feeding of the 5,000, and on and on.

But Jesus thought small that night. He got out a towel and a basin, placed himself in the role of a servant, and washed the feet of the disciples. He was a busboy again. The significance of this was not lost on Peter. When it dawned on him that Jesus was doing the small gesture instead of a big gesture—much like Mother Teresa picking up one dying woman—Peter understood what Jesus was asking of him.

"Not just my feet," he said, "but my hands and my head as well!" (John 13:9, NIV).

It was a small thing that ended up covering, and transforming, the disciple.

Michael Pitts, one of the volunteers on our Calcutta airlift, had an extraordinary experience during a mass with Mother Teresa on one of our last days there. We had all visited orphanages, clinics, and leprosy villages; and he and his wife, Suzanne, had also worked in the Home for Dying Destitutes, feeding and bathing those who were in their final days with nowhere else to go.

> When our hands are extended in service to one another, they are larger than life.

Just before we arrived in Calcutta, Mother Teresa had fallen and broken her collarbone, so she was spending much of her time in bed trying to recover. But she had the strength to celebrate a mass with us at the end. She said she wanted to give us a blessing.

"When she reached up to put her hand on my head, I

thought, 'This tiny woman's hands are huge!'" Michael said. "It felt as if her hand covered my entire head."

You see, this diminutive, frail, old lady's hands had been doing small things for so long that, when extended, they seemed larger than life. When our hands extend in service to one another, they *are* larger than life. They give life. And meaning. And purpose. And hope.

Margaret Mead said, "Never doubt that a small group of thoughtful, committed citizens can change the world; indeed, it's the only thing that ever has." And while I agree wholeheartedly with her, it is important to remember that we don't think small merely because we think it is going to lead to something else. This is an impure motive. Responding to the need of that moment is enough. We can't know if our actions have implications for the future, and we don't concern ourselves with knowing.

The people who took Steve Lamb's kids to Little League practice haven't mobilized, bought a fleet of vans or school buses, and started a global athletic transportation network. They didn't have to. They did small things with great love. Busboy kinds of things. That was enough.

The Journey

We don't know where our work with Heart to Heart will take us. We didn't know that after going to Belize, we would go to St. Croix, or that we would go to Calcutta, Armenia, Vietnam, China, or anywhere else. We didn't plan any project with bigger things in mind. We did each one because we sensed that it was what we should do at the time. Our goal has never been to be big, but to be effective.

People often ask us where we think the Heart to Heart organization is headed. I have no idea. The destination isn't our priority. It's the journey. It's whatever is next. If anyone had asked Mother Teresa, at any time during her work, where she saw her efforts heading, she would have answered, "To the next person who needs us." Isn't that enough?

Are we doing all we can with what we have? I regularly ask our staff. Success for us is not how big, or well known, or recognized we are. It is in knowing that we did what we could with what we had.

I have taken care of a lot of patients at the end of their lives when they knew they were in their final days. No one has ever told me that they wished they had made more money, or run for public office, or tried harder to get that promotion at work, or followed through on one more project. No one has said that they wish they had thought bigger. Many, though, have said that they wish they had used their lives to help others. That's one of the most frequent, and saddest, regrets I hear.

When you visit a nursing home, look at what the residents have hanging on their walls. It's easy to see what is really important to them. Pictures of family, a crayon drawing from a grandchild, maybe a cross. I rarely see pictures of houses, a list of assets, or a company plaque.

Life isn't about big stuff. It isn't accomplishments.

Mother Teresa wasn't thinking that picking up a dying woman off the street would be the means to starting Missions of Charity around the world.

Steve Lamb's neighbors weren't thinking that they were onto a huge service project that would include thousands of children.

And surely Jesus wasn't thinking that, once He did that water into wine miracle, it would lead to resurrections.

Life isn't about big stuff. It isn't accomplishments.

It's small stuff. Stuff that is done by someone for someone else. The only stuff that matters.

4

WHEN THE NIGHTMARES STOPPED

TERRY WATERS HATED THE VIETNAMESE. AS A MEMber of a special military unit during the Vietnam War, he fought them face-to-face, conducting secret reconnaissance missions in areas where, if caught, he would have been tortured or killed, and his presence in those areas would have been denied by the U.S. government.

He hated them so much that, when his first tour of duty ended, he immediately signed up for another one. Then another. He faced many near-death situations, and each one fed his ego. He was superb at what he did. Occasionally, though, he needed a little extra help to keep his confidence up. To get him through certain missions, he began using the high-quality heroin produced in Southeast Asia. "Why not?" he thought. "I will probably be dead tomorrow."

Near the end of his time in Vietnam, something happened that changed the course of his life. He was scheduled as the point man for a nighttime mission. But a few hours before the sun went down, this highly trained stealth soldier fell into a trench on his nice, safe base, and hurt himself. Someone needed to replace him on the mission. His friend Bill Bonner volunteered.

That night, Terry listened on the radio, his leg bandaged, as the team moved through the mountains. He listened with anticipation, knowing that it was a mission he was supposed to lead. Suddenly the silence and the occasional squelches of the radio were replaced with sounds of explosions, gunfire, and screams.

Terry's friend Bill had tripped a land mine, killing him instantly, setting off an ambush by enemy soldiers. Nearly everyone in Terry's team was killed.

Terry tried to stifle his rage by using more drugs. Stronger drugs. His hatred became so great that, after he had returned to the United States, he would cross the street to avoid a Vietnamese person for fear of what he might do. His drug abuse finally led him to treatment through a Veterans Administration hospital, but he simply replaced one drug for another—alcohol. The rage and drug abuse went on for years.

> Terry's friend Bill had tripped a land mine, killing him instantly, setting off an ambush by enemy soldiers.

He hit bottom in Florida.

He found God in 1987, and the tragedy of Bill Bonner's death did what no sermon illustration or Sunday School lesson could. He knew his life needed a purpose. He knew he didn't want to waste what had been spared. Two years later he fell in love with a woman named Lan. Unbelievably, she was Vietnamese.

Terry's life soon took an even bigger turn. Lan, who fled Saigon when it fell to the North Vietnamese, had felt for years that she was supposed to return to Vietnam to work with her people. She had a desire in her heart to provide medicine to the poor and sick of her country, but she hadn't seen how it was possible.

She shared her dream with Terry, who, again, was surprised by his response. Instead of dismissing the idea as prolonging the lives of the enemy, he felt drawn to it. Soon they made plans to go to Ho Chi Minh City to work with Lan's aunt in the Red Cross.

For six months they worked as volunteers in a leprosy village, home to 300 diseased and dying Vietnamese, and they worked through the Red Cross in other hospitals, clinics, and orphanages. They also dealt with local merchants to provide rice to the facilities. Despite their contributions, Lan was never satisfied because her vision of providing medicine had not been fulfilled.

As their time in Vietnam began to wind down, Terry and Lan tried to think of ways to remain; but the money they had set aside for this volunteer venture was about gone, with no prospects of finding a source of income there. Somewhat discouraged, they decided to return to the U.S.

Just a few weeks before their departure, though, Lan received a telephone call from Barbi Moore, who worked with Heart to Heart. They had never met, didn't know each other's background, hadn't shared any dreams. Heart to Heart had been looking for a way to conduct an airlift to Vietnam but didn't know anyone there. For days Barbi had called people in the U.S., asking if anyone had a contact in Vietnam. Someone told her about Terry and Lan.

It all made sense to Lan. The Waterses' network with the Red Cross, the leprosy village, the clinics, the merchants, were all in place. Of course she and Terry would help make the airlift happen, she said.

They canceled their departure plans.

There were some substantial hurdles to get over. It had been 20 years since a commercial U.S. plane had flown into Vietnam. The two countries had been conducting their own cold war since 1975. It wasn't a matter of just asking if a planeload of medical supplies and pharmaceuticals could come in. A 20-year glacier had to thaw.

This thawing didn't even seem possible when I first suggested the idea of an airlift 3 years earlier. The reception from everyone I talked with then had been icy indeed. But in 1994 I went to Hanoi to present the idea to several government leaders. I suggested having the airlift occur during the 20th anniversary of the U.S. troop pullout as a way to symbolize the goodwill of the American people and to provide a catalyst in the healing between our nations.

Soon it had the support of both governments. Senator Kit Bond from Missouri wanted to go with us. The Vietnam ambassador to the U.S. supported it. Corporations got behind it too. Federal Express supplied the plane, McDonnell Douglas donated money and a great deal of technical and logistical assistance, and Black and Veatch, an engineering firm, donated money, office space in Vietnam, and more logistical support. Pharmaceutical companies donated medicines and medical supplies.

To make the airlift a reality, though, Heart to Heart needed permission from the Vietnamese government for rights to fly into Vietnam airspace—a request that had not been granted for two decades; landing rights for both Ho Chi Minh City and Hanoi; permission from Vietnam Customs to bring in the medicines and supplies; a waiver of all landing and fueling fees; permission to transport supplies from one city to another; permission to talk with the news media; permission to stay in people's homes; permission to take pictures; and permission to move around freely. All of these permissions first needed the approval of then prime minister, Vo Van Kiet. We asked Lan what she thought she could do.

> At first, members of the Communist government were not favorable toward the proposal ... The government had planned a massive celebration to commemorate what they called the "Victory over the Americans."

A Family Reunion

Lan thought of her uncles—relatives she had not seen or spoken to in years—and remembered that they worked in the central government, reporting directly to the prime minister. She decided that it was time for a family reunion.

At first, members of the Communist government were not

favorable toward the proposal that the Waterses were carrying for us. The government had planned a massive celebration to commemorate what they called the "Victory over the Americans." They were reluctant to have something occur during that time that could detract from the atmosphere. A U.S.-based mission of reconciliation and compassion didn't initially fit the plan.

But Terry and Lan persisted. Lan asked an uncle, a retired general in the Vietnamese army, for help. She showed him the list of six sites in the north and six in the south that would receive these tons of medicines. Her uncle directed Lan and Terry to another uncle—someone the Waterses had never met—who worked directly for the prime minister.

Lan said that this uncle laughed at her request and said, "You're not asking for much, are you?" Yet in three days we had the letter from the prime minister. All permissions were granted shortly after that.

Hanoi and Ho Chi Minh City

The day before the cargo plane arrived, I flew into Hanoi and was amazed to see a giant banner hanging from the terminal welcoming Heart to Heart. On the drive from the airport to the hotel, I saw two billboards with the same welcome. That night the deputy minister of foreign affairs hosted a dinner for about 20 guests—including Senator Bond, the U.S. liaison to Vietnam, the U.S. Army colonel in charge of MIA operations, and executives of some of our major airlift sponsors.

There was the usual nervous conversation at first, some toasts, several welcomes, and then dinner. I spent most of my time talking with the deputy foreign minister, and we both expressed how much we wanted to put the past behind us and look to a brighter future.

Soon we were talking about our children and his grandchildren, and where we grew up. There were more similarities than differences. Eventually it felt as if we were distant relatives of the same family.

The next day when that huge MD-11 Federal Express plane emerged out of the overcast sky and screamed its presence on the runway, tears flowed freely among both Americans and Vietnamese, because it symbolized a new day of friendship between our two countries.

The significance was not lost on the news media, either. Most international news organizations were already in Vietnam doing stories on the 20th anniversary of the end of the war. They saw that, with the Heart to Heart airlift, something else was taking the place of the war.

The significance wasn't that the U.S. decided to sponsor an airlift or that Congress voted an appropriation—they didn't. It was significant because ordinary people decided that they would do something extraordinary to symbolize the love and friendship of Americans to Vietnamese. The result was $7 million in donated medicines and supplies.

As a doctor, I know how unhealthy it is to let a wound fester. There has been untold suffering on both sides. Wounds are supposed to heal.

We unloaded part of the plane in Hanoi, then took the rest of the supplies to Ho Chi Minh City. Through contacts made by Terry and Lan, we were able to tour several hospitals and Red Cross centers. A CNN crew was waiting for us when we arrived at the first site, and stayed with us for much of the day. Our lunch was sponsored by the Red Cross at a small Vietnamese hotel. The owner of the hotel had heard me comment that Heart to Heart was almost entirely a volunteer organization, and he "volunteered" our lunch for us!

Rice by the Ton

The best part of the trip was our visit to a rural leprosy village. More than 80 families in which at least one parent has the disease live there. Most of the families have children, so there were more than 300 people living in this isolated camp.

The majority live in simple mud-floored, reed and bamboo huts. Others share barracks-type buildings with several families. The government provides $8 per family per month to feed and operate the village, which does not cover the basic needs.

When we saw that the people were hungry, Barbi went

with the village leaders to the nearest town to buy some rice. The village officials took her to the part of the market where the cheapest brown rice was sold. Barbi let some of the dry, gnarled grains run through her fingers, and she said, "Don't you have anything better than this?" They took her to the section where the quality rice was sold.

"We'll take a ton of this," she said.

The village leaders looked as if they had been shot.

"You would buy this for lepers?"

At the village we handed each family several large bags of rice. Then we asked the children to come forward and gave each one a pencil and a pad of paper. Their gratitude was overwhelming.

People who live in a leprosy village look as gruesome as you might imagine. Some have parts of their faces missing. The disease devours body parts indiscriminately. The village leader, who was very old, had lost all his fingers and toes. Six weeks before our arrival he had collapsed from a stroke; now he could hardly speak. When he heard that our group was coming to his village, and that there was a priest among us, he asked to be returned to his small hut. He was lying on a reed mat—the right side of his body was paralyzed—when we arrived.

> *The village leader, who was very old, had lost all his fingers and toes.*

The chief motioned for us to pray for him. Fr. Gene Arthur, a member of our delegation, is a Jesuit priest, and he grasped the man's deformed hand and blessed him and prayed for him. Members of the village peered in through the open door and windows; they weren't used to seeing people pray like this, and they weren't used to being touched.

Is leprosy contagious? We didn't care. Love is. Hope is.

The intense emotion of the day continued when we traveled to the Tu Doc Prosthetics Center to fit more than 100 amputees with donated prosthetic legs. A Reuters TV crew was waiting for us, and they stayed for the entire encounter. The clinic staff asked us to help strap the limbs on the patients. Several double amputees were there for the wheelchairs we brought, and we got to lift them onto their new chairs. Most of these patients had been injured in the war more than 20 years before. Finally, they were able to begin to move on. So were several in our delegation, in a different way.

We also visited several hospitals, with the most memorable one an obstetrics and gynecology facility. The staff there performs 6,000 high-risk deliveries per year, plus gynecologic surgery. The delivery room was spartan, with four delivery tables in one room. Two patients were delivering while we walked through.

The operating room had two tables, also both in one room. There was a rack of drying surgical gloves, which they wash and reuse over and over. The neonatal intensive care unit was full of babies in isolettes—many with two and three babies packed into each tiny isolette.

The war didn't cause all of this. Leprosy and overcrowded incubators aren't the fault of Americans. But we have more than we need. And some members of our extended human family, made in the image of God, don't have enough.

Our visit to Vietnam was memorable because we helped build a bridge of peace between enemies, embraced the untouchable, provided lifesaving medicine to the dying, and brought mobility to the limbless. But our final night there was memorable for a different reason.

Dinner was a nine-course meal of various snake dishes.

As we walked through the courtyard of the private home where we were about to have our last meal with our new family members—a meal given as a gesture of highest honor—we saw the main course in its natural state as it slithered across the ground. It was cobra night in Hanoi!

The cooks caught the snakes and slit their throats, draining their blood into tiny glasses. The gallbladder was dissected out, and the bile fluid was drained into another container. Then they skinned the snakes.

Dinner was a nine-course meal of various snake dishes. It started with a taste of cobra blood, then of bile fluid. And since I was chairman of Heart to Heart, I was presented with the raw and still-beating heart. I considered changing our name on the spot! I asked for a knife and sliced the heart into several pieces so everyone could share in the honor.

Then we ate snake soup, fried snake, grilled snake, snake skin fritters, snake liver, snake egg rolls, and for dessert, snake and corn chowder.

We didn't know beforehand that a strong stomach was a prerequisite for this project!

Vietnam: When the Nightmares Stopped

Vietnam wasn't our biggest airlift, but it was the most historic. It involved many firsts: the first commercial American plane to land in Vietnam since the war; the first U.S. flag to fly in Hanoi; the first airlift of its kind to Vietnam; the largest private humanitarian project in Vietnam to date. But it was more than that. Over and over again, U.S. State Department officials and business and civic leaders told us that they had never seen such openness and cooperation from the two governments.

It was also one of the important catalysts in bringing former enemies back together. Terry and Lan Waters remained in Vietnam for a while after we left to make sure the medicines reached their destinations. At one major site the medicine was divided for 13 substations in outlying rural areas. Terry and Lan traveled for several hours up small tributaries—formerly patrolled by gunboats—to deliver the materials.

The wounds of Terry and Lan had begun healing before our airlift. Not so for the wounds of Art Fillmore, which were still festering.

Art is also a combat veteran from the Vietnam War. As a member of the 25th Infantry Division in 1969, he patrolled along the Vietnam/Cambodian border, spending considerable time in or near the city of Cu Chi. He was in countless firefights

with Vietnam guerrillas who, soon after appearing and shooting, would suddenly disappear through their sophisticated
miles-long tunnel system.

When he returned to the United States, he turned the horror of his experience inward, talking with few people about his
encounters. The encounters visited him, though, in the form of
nightmares—and they were similar each night.

His recurring dream was that he was being sent back to
fight in Vietnam; and once he
got there, a ghoulish creature
would greet him and read from
a script the names of all the people Art saw killed or limbs
blown off during the war. The
ghoul terrified him regularly for
nearly 25 years.

His recurring dream
was that he was
being sent back to fight in
Vietnam; and once he
got there, a ghoulish creature
would greet him . . .

The way I met Art was un-
usual. His partner in a Kansas
City law firm was traveling in
Vietnam and met Mother Teresa
on an Easter Sunday. When he
told her that he was from
Kansas City, she said that she
had been in contact with a
Kansas City group called Heart to Heart International. Since I
had visited with her previously and had started working out
the details for an airlift to Calcutta, she knew all about us. She
told him to look me up.

When he returned to Kansas City, he called to arrange a
meeting with Art Fillmore and me.

Art told me a little about his experiences in Vietnam and
his subsequent nightmares, and I suggested that he go with us
on the Vietnam airlift. His reply was simple: "Yeah, and I want
to go through another divorce too."

But he listened and asked more questions, and said he
would give it some more thought. Finally he told me, "Maybe
this would be a good way to deal with the ghosts."

It was a haunting experience for him to go to Hanoi, be-

cause it was at the Hanoi Hilton where so many American prisoners of war had been kept and tortured. His Vietnamese host
asked him if he wanted to visit a museum dedicated to the war.
It was in a city called Cu Chi.

"I took a duffel bag of medicine this time," he said. "It was
better to do that than carry an M-16 or call in an air strike."

Visiting the museum was difficult because it glorified the
Vietcong resistance, and Art was happy to leave. Next stop that
day was a hospital in Cu Chi.

The doctor giving him the tour asked if he had been in
Vietnam before, which is the code for asking if he had been in
the war. Art told him that he had, and named some tiny villages
in the area. The doctor stopped the hospital tour and took Art
for a ride.

They traveled along the same river that Art had patrolled,
saw the same villages, and walked in areas that he had been
part of and where he had witnessed massive killing and destruction.

"I saw the kids playing, people working in fields, and it
dawned on me that these people weren't my enemy anymore,"
he said. "They were just like me. It was the first time I had
sensed that kind of serenity."

They returned to the hospital, where the doctor showed
him a boy suffering from a kidney disease. His abdomen was
swollen, and he was in extreme pain. Art asked how the doctor
was treating the boy, and the doctor showed him an array of
herbal medicine.

Art reached into his duffel bag and started pulling out boxes.

"Will anything in here help?" he asked.

The doctor picked up a box of antibiotics and looked directly at the child's father.

"Your boy's going to live," he announced.

Art, the doctor, and the boy's father responded with hugs
and tears.

And Art's nightmares stopped.

He has been back to Vietnam a few more times and is even
able to joke about parts of it. At a dinner there, he was seated
across from the country's vice minister of agriculture; and as the

conversation developed, they realized they had actually been in combat against one another.

"Lucky for me you were a bad shot!" joked the government official. "Likewise!" Art replied.

Since those trips Art has had a spiritual renewal too. He said that for the first time since the war, in the confusion over what to do with his spared life, he has a purpose. He looks for ways he can relieve suffering. He has dreams, not nightmares. His recent baptism, he told me, was one of the most exciting days of his life.

We were convinced all along that the inspiration for this project was from God. That belief was confirmed when it matched Lan Waters's vision from years ago. She had no idea why she felt she would be delivering medicine to her people after the war. She and Terry were simply faithful to what they believed was of God.

It made sense later, of course, when Barbi Moore called. The Red Cross network was in place, getting ready for an airlift they didn't know was coming. This is consistent with the experience we have had on virtually every project. We have found people who have our same passion for serving the poor and needy—Rotarians, caring businesspeople, local companies, government and civic leaders, religious leaders. People respond, the projects get done, and lives are improved.

Not Eye to Eye, but Shoulder to Shoulder

It's a powerful thing to replace hate with love. Just ask Terry Waters. Or Art Fillmore.

Or ask the people who sat around the conference table at Heart to Heart in Kansas City once a month for a year, arguing about how to conduct an airlift to Bosnia for victims of the devastating civil war there.

We wanted the cooperation of the ethnic, religious, and political groups involved, so we gathered representatives from Serbia and Croatia, along with those from Muslim, Catholic, Protestant, Jewish, and Orthodox faiths to meet regularly to discuss the project.

There was more yelling, name-calling, and table pounding

among these adults than any group of kids I've encountered. Each one militantly wanted the shipment to go to his or her group exclusively, which fired the anger of the others. I half-expected one of them to say, "If you won't do the airlift my way, I'm going to take my sick and dying people and go home."

Here's what they did say: "Each group should collect their own medicines and supplies, and pick their own recipients. All money raised by each group should go to that group's hospitals."

Everyone was worried that some other group was going to get more than its share. Many around the table were emphatic that we shouldn't help the Serbians, that they couldn't be trusted, and that we should drop them from the project.

I kept saying that the most important thing was not the pills, but the fact that we were doing this together, as a family. Each meeting lasted for hours; at the end of each one, our staff, exhausted and frustrated, was convinced that it had been the death-blow to the project. "They'll never come back after *that* meeting," our staff would say.

Then the next month they'd be back; we'd go over more details and have more discussion, and then it would deteriorate all over again into yelling and name-calling. Over the din of one meeting I finally banged my fist on the conference table and said at full volume, "The medicines will go to the greatest needs regardless of who collected them and regardless of what political group they represent!"

> I thought that would change their minds.
>
> I thought silence would come over us, then shame would set in, followed by an outpouring of unity.
>
> But it didn't.

"But they are the enemy!" shouted one of the men at the table.

I tried to think of something profound to say. The words of Jesus came to mind.

"What about 'Love your enemies'?" I responded (Matt. 5:44; Luke 6:27, 35).

I thought that would change their minds. I thought silence would come over us, then shame would set in, followed by an outpouring of unity. But it didn't. They just kept bickering.

It was near Christmastime, and the meeting was coming to a conclusion, with no apparent progress. It looked as if the airlift was not going to happen, because if we couldn't get the cooperation of the groups in the U.S., we surely wouldn't get it in Bosnia.

As the meeting broke up, each person became a little more civil and wished the other a happy holiday. Getting their coats on, they inquired about each other's families, and the talk turned to children. The more they talked about their children, and about each other's children, the more pleasant they became with one another. Then they wished each other's families well, and you could see it dawn on each of them what was happening.

Soon they had their coats off again and were around the table, invigorated and committed to finding a solution to our differences over how to provide relief to this war-torn region. They decided to do it for each other's children.

At a later press conference announcing the airlift, Rabbi Mark Levin of Congregation Beth Torah said, "We have not always seen eye to eye on this project, but we see that we can work shoulder to shoulder, and heart to heart, for the children of Sarajevo."

The project was on!

Within months we sent a convoy of supplies, under military protection, to that devastated area. We were warned of robbery and the need for lots of cash to bribe the guards. Neither possibility materialized. For a brief time, for a common purpose, enemies united for the sake of the needy.

Responding to the Need—No Matter What

Since the fall of the Soviet Union, one of the U.S.'s longest-standing enemies has been North Korea. The Korean war ended more than 40 years ago, but we continue to peer across the border of South Korea, guns aimed and cocked.

The idea for a project to North Korea grew out of our airlift to Calcutta. One of the people we worked with there was Vijai Singh, from New Delhi. Mr. Singh had religious training at a seminary in South Korea nearly 20 years ago and, like Lan Waters, sensed a vision years before our visit. His vision involved helping the people of North Korea.

For 17 years he had applied for a visa to that country and was rejected each time. He was discouraged and confused about this burden, but he hadn't forgotten it.

North Korea and India are not political enemies, so they have embassies in each other's countries. Mr. Singh regularly visited the North Korean embassy to befriend the employees there. It was the least he could do, he thought, since he couldn't actually get into the country.

One day North Korean embassy officials visited Mr. Singh at his home and told him of the severe starvation in their country after months of rain and flooding had wiped out their harvests. Did he have contacts with anyone who could help? they asked.

The idea for a project to North Korea grew out of our airlift to Calcutta.

He told them about Heart to Heart, and that we would be arriving in India soon. So they asked to meet with us while we were there. One of the volunteers in our delegation had lived in South Korea, so when we all met at Mr. Singh's house, they were delighted to hear their own language spoken. By the end of the meal they invited all of us to come to North Korea, including Mr. Singh. He had been begging the North Korean government for permission to enter their country for 17 years without success. Now the government was asking him to come.

We brought in a shipment of grain and $1 million worth of medicine.

North Korea was far different from what I expected. I had been to the USSR before its fall, and to Romania, Albania, Vietnam, and other Communist countries. Most were the same— poor, decaying, disorderly, chaotic, dark, and streets full of depressed people without hope. This place, though, was a total surprise. Apartment buildings in Pyongyang were 30 to 40 stories high. Our hotel was in two towers, each 45 stories tall. In the middle of downtown is a Christmas-tree-shaped hotel that is 105 stories tall!

But what was even more surprising was the lack of people on the sidewalks and streets. Downtown was spotless and empty. The only people we saw were soldiers.

The skyscrapers were punctuated by massive public buildings, stadiums, libraries, auditoriums, along with plenty of green parks. There were no billboards or advertising. It was the cleanest, emptiest city I had ever seen.

We toured some of their hospitals where our medicines were being used. The Pyongyang Medical University Hospital was a large, 1,000-bed multispecialty hospital that trains 4,000 students in various health care fields. It was organized, clean, and well equipped. We saw a variety of nuclear medicine and sonography equipment, for instance.

Another facility we visited was the Maternity Hospital, which is actually a women's and pediatric hospital. It has 1,500 beds and treats a wide variety of women's diseases. It also performs 25,000 deliveries each year, with a C-section rate of only 5 percent. The lobby had beautiful marble floors and a giant crystal chandelier.

The natural disasters of the previous three years were unprecedented in North Korea's history.

Both hospitals were quite modern, and the doctors showed us how they were using the medicines we had provided. The medical staff was quite knowledgeable in how to use them and expressed their gratitude several times. On the equipment side they were in good shape. They were grateful for the medicine.

But what the country *really* needed was food.

The natural disasters of the previous three years were unprecedented in North Korea's history. A severe hailstorm in 1994, a devastating flood in 1995, and just as they were trying to recover, another major flood that wiped out most of what was left of the rice crop. Even though they tried not to act too desperate publicly, they were secretly begging for help.

The director of the Flood Damage Rehabilitation Committee said that the rice ration had been cut from 600 grams per day (about 2,400 calories) to much less, although he wouldn't be specific when I tried to pin him down.

When I told a business group in the U.S. about our shipment to North Korea, the questions flew at me: Didn't I know that they were Communists? Didn't I know that they were the enemy? Didn't I know that we considered dropping an atomic bomb on them? Didn't I know that they were a constant threat to our ally South Korea?

They accused Heart to Heart of being too political, something that has never been said about the organization before or since. Some of them threatened to cancel their financial support of our projects.

It seems to me that being political is when you do things for certain people because of whose side they are on, and you don't do things for certain people who are on the other side. From my perspective, the action of the business group was political, not ours. Responding to people because of their need is not political.

In Calcutta a group representing starving people asked for help, and we had the means to provide donated food and medicine. Looking them in the eye, I could not ask if they were members of the Communist Party. All that mattered was that they were hungry.

Jesus said that there is nothing unusual about people looking after their own kind. Tax gatherers and sinners do that, He said. What's extraordinary is that we're told to do more: "Love your enemies."

The result of taking these words seriously is that Terry Waters still helps preserve lives in a country where he learned to hate and kill. Art Fillmore's nightmares of terror were replaced by a spirit of love. Serbian, Croatian, Jewish, Muslim, and other religious enemies joined hands around a conference table to pray for each other's people and for each other's children. North Koreans asked for, and received, help from their American "enemies."

And Lan Waters and Mr. Singh got to see the fulfillment of visions they felt they were given—to help specific groups of needy, unpopular people.

This command to love our enemies is radical. It erases political boundaries and forces us to look at people, not politics. That may be one of the most revolutionary concepts in history and may hold more power to resolve differences than we dare admit.

5

MIDGETS IN A WORLD OF SMALL THINGS

CALCUTTA HAS A BILLBOARD YOU WOULDN'T BELIEVE. You've been to cities where the sign welcoming you says, Home of the Largest Man-eating Clam, or Watermelon Capital of the World. Maybe the signs you have seen have had a welcome from the local Rotary Club or the Knights of Columbus, or maybe they have lists of the churches you can choose.

In San Diego a sign says, Welcome to America's Finest City. It doesn't tell who gave San Diego that designation, but the declaration is there, nonetheless.

Other cities promote their sports franchises, their natural resources, their industry, their work ethic, or their famous sons and daughters.

Garrison Keillor, storyteller and radio host, has a slogan for his fictional town, Lake Wobegon, Minnesota: "Where all the women are strong, the men are good-looking, and the children are above average."

Calcutta, one of India's largest cities, has a billboard that would not meet the approval of any chamber of commerce I know. It says, Welcome to Calcutta—the City of Filth, Hunger, Warmth, Smiles, and Joy! How's that for a combination?

I'll never forget the first time I visited Calcutta. It overwhelmed me. The sight of all that need was something I had never experienced in one location before. The heat, the noise, and the pollution combine into a sensory overload. The smell got my teenage daughter's attention immediately. "It's a collection of death, feces, and rotting food," she said. I have to agree.

But by no means does that mean it is repulsive. Something about all of that assault on one's senses is beckoning. Maybe it is because I met Mother Teresa during that first visit. Her heart for the needs of others is contagious. After my first visit with her I decided that someday, if I ever had the chance, I would try to do something to help the work of Mother Teresa and the Missionaries of Charity. This was way before Heart to Heart.

More than 10 years later I got that chance and returned with about 90 volunteers and 50 tons of medicine worth $12 million. A dream that started with seeing overwhelming need mushroomed into a giant airlift that responded to that need.

A Divine Encounter

During our airlift to Calcutta each of us worked in different facilities for a few days. Most of the facilities were part of Mother Teresa's Missionaries of Charity. As I mentioned, Suzanne Pitts, one of our staff, worked in the Nirmal Hriday, which means Home for Dying Destitutes.

Suzanne was apprehensive going to work there—but not because she has a weak stomach. She wondered if she could do anything that would make a difference.

The home is an old concrete building jammed in with several others on the block, surrounded by narrow streets filled with merchants, rickshas, beggars, and lung-seizing dust.

The nuns in the Home for Dying Destitutes dress in sparkling white with blue trim and stand out in sharp contrast to the dirt and grime of Calcutta. They showed Suzanne the men's and women's wards—each with approximately 40 people. The dying were on cots about three feet apart. Each cot was covered by a coarse green sheet, and each person wore a light-colored

The home is a place that strips away all pretense and instantly destroys false views of self and humanity.

gown. Painted on the wall above each cot was a number, 1
through 40.

Because everyone in that house has dysentery, the cots are
just inches off the floor to make it easier to clean them and the
patients. The home is a place that strips away all pretense and
instantly destroys false views of self and humanity.

Suzanne's tasks included helping with the cooking, laun-
dry, and the one-on-one personal care for the dying. The concrete floor was scrubbed clean, and the most dominant smell in
the building was of disinfectant.

Alongside the sisters, Suzanne scrubbed, scalded, disinfect-
ed, and rinsed the towering mounds of soiled sheets and gowns
that must be cleaned frequently. She felt like a wimp, she said,
in her heavy-duty yellow plastic gloves as she toiled alongside
the bare-handed sisters.

She worked at a variety of tasks, which included bathing
patients, helping dress wounds, and attempting to comfort patients—most of whom did not speak English. Somewhere during the day her gloves went by the wayside.

One patient could not be comforted, and wailed intermit-
tently.

At lunchtime, Suzanne and the sisters helped feed those
who could eat. The meal was rice, vegetables, a bit of fish, and a
small tangerine.

It was then, she says, that she had an encounter with the
Divine.

After helping one woman eat what she could, Suzanne
looked about the ward to see who else needed assistance. One
row of cots was placed on a wide concrete ledge raised about
three feet higher than the main floor. In the upper right-hand
corner of this row she saw a tiny, wizened lady of an indeterminable age perched on her cot with her knees awkwardly
drawn to her chest. Her plate was on the cot in front of her.

Even from a distance Suzanne could see the woman's mis-
shapen hands, and that she was having great difficulty with the
simple task of feeding herself.

Her arthritis was so bad that it looked as if she were a mari-
onette, and her puppeteer had drawn the strings in tightly so

that she was almost circular, ready to be put in the traveling
trunk. Every movement contorted her face. Her 80-pound body
was in constant pain.

Suzanne went to her side and asked if she could help. Very
graciously, and in her cultured British accent, she declined
Suzanne's offer but said she could sit and talk with her while
she ate.

Her name was Lucy, and she had been an orphan since she
was very young. She was brought to the Missionaries of Charity, who raised and educated her. They were her family, she said.

Very laboriously and with clearly painful movements, Lucy
slowly fed herself a portion of the meal on her bed. She allowed
Suzanne to help her peel and separate slices of the tangerine,
and then she offered some to those on the cots near her.

She told Suzanne that she spent most of her life elsewhere,
but seven years ago developed this crippling arthritis. She returned to the sisters and has lived in a home like this since then,
because there was no one else to care for her. Seven years she'd
been there with the dying as she felt her own body grow more
rigid and less under her control, with every movement increasing in pain.

The Missionaries of Charity prepared her for life, and now
they were preparing her for death. She was back among the
poorest of the poor.

As she talked with Suzanne, she would stop frequently and
intently scan the rows of the ward, her deep-set brown eyes
filled with zealous concern. From her elevated vantage point
she could see each woman lying on her bed of private pain.

Then a startling, booming voice would come out of that
frail, frozen body. "Sister, Sister," she called out. "Number 34
needs you." A sister responded quickly, comforted the woman
in cot 34, then nodded in acknowledgment to Lucy before moving on to other women.

Suzanne thought back over the morning and remembered
hearing that voice call several other times to the one sister trying to care for all 40 women. It was as if she were the sister's assistant, alerting her to desperate needs that the sister would not
otherwise know about.

"Lucy," Suzanne began awkwardly, wanting to convey her respect for Lucy's invaluable contribution to the residents of the house. "I have noticed what you do, and . . . well, I think it's wonderful."

Lucy sat very still and didn't speak for several moments. Finally she turned her face to Suzanne, her eyes burning into her guest's, and spoke in a quiet voice filled with dignity.

"Jesus has given me eyes and a voice, and I will use them for Him," she said in a near whisper. "Someday when I can no longer do this, someone will do it for me."

> "Jesus has given me eyes and a voice, and I will use them for Him," she said in a near whisper.

The raucous noise of the city outside and the moanings of the dying humanity inside the building stilled. A divine encounter was being etched on Suzanne's heart. "Listen," Suzanne said to herself. "And remember. Listen. God is speaking to you."

"My spirit felt the nearness of the Sacred," Suzanne said later.

Soon Suzanne had to leave that holy place. She and Lucy agreed to pray for one another.

"Her witness and determination to use the resources God gave her are alive in my heart," Suzanne says. "The gift she gave continues to give me peace. It humbles me, and inspires me to live out the call on my life."

Who would have thought that, in a roomful of death, Lucy's abilities could still bring peace and comfort? She is only one person. All she had left were her eyes and her voice, but they were still useful.

If any person ever had a reason to complain about the unfairness of life, it was Lucy. But she didn't complain. She continues to give of herself to care for those around her.

Be the One

Years ago General Motors conducted a quality improvement campaign with a slogan, "It Only Takes One." One sales representative could increase sales. One manufacturing employee could improve the car as it passed on the assembly line. One accountant could increase efficiency. And if a lot of those "ones" really believed that each person could improve the performance of the company, then the company would improve, according to the campaign.

As a reminder, the company handed out pins that employees could stick on their collars, lapels, or sleeves. It was simply the number 1. It didn't say GM, or "It Only Takes One." It was just a 1. But every time employees looked at it, they would be reminded that, not only did it only take one, but also who the 1 was: themselves. They were the one.

Sometimes meetings would end with managers saying, "Be the One."

Norm Shoemaker, one of the volunteers who went with us on our airlift to China, has been my friend for a long time. I first heard him tell about this campaign years ago. He was traveling, saw the "1" on a man's lapel, and asked him about it. Later Norm thought about the campaign and felt that it had broader implications than just increasing car sales. He wondered what would happen if people really believed that they—as individuals—were capable of "Being the One," to make a difference in the lives of someone else. So now Norm ends many of his conversations by saying, "Be the One." In other words, "You Can Make a Difference."

Using what we have to help someone else is what gives our lives meaning and gives the world hope.

I really like that slogan. My own interpretation is that everyone has something to offer, no matter how small. Everyone has something to give. God can use everybody in a special and unique place where someone has a need. Using what we have to help someone else is what gives our lives meaning and gives the world hope. My phrase isn't as crisp as General Motors', but it is, simply, "Do What You Can." Even if what you can do is small. Can it get much smaller than what Lucy had to give?

Virtually everyone who has gone with us on one of our airlifts has come to the conclusion that they can truly "Be the One." They see it when they are involved in these extraordinary needs, and they see it in the small things when they return home.

Diane Bosworth, a stay-at-home mom, went on the airlift to Calcutta. At the outset she felt intimidated and useless, surrounded by people she deemed more qualified to be on the project. A member of the rock band Queen had come. The senior vice president of Federal Express was there, along with executives from McDonnell Douglas, attorneys, doctors, government officials, and dozens of other professionals who volunteered to help distribute the medicines and work in the clinics.

"What am I doing here?" she said while we were en route. "I am only a mother. All of these other people can *do* something. I only know how to be a mom."

She hadn't heard the "Be the One" speech, and, frankly, I don't know that she would have believed it. Someone telling her that being a mother was in itself honorable, and that she was more than that anyway, would not have convinced her.

She felt like a midget in a world of small things.

Most of that feeling of worthlessness went by the wayside once we started unloading the airplane and distributing the supplies to the various clinics. But it *all* made sense to her in a hospital wing that was mostly for babies—babies who were not expected to live.

A sign on the wall said, in big letters, Please Do Not Hold the Babies.

Diane asked a nurse about the sign.

"Because if you hold one baby, the others see that, and they all start crying because they want to be held," was the matter-of-fact reply. "So we don't hold any of them."

Babies who can't be held? Just lying there? Untouched in some cases until after they die and are removed from their overcrowded beds? It was unfathomable to Diane.

So she held them. All of them.

"After all," she said, "I am a mother."

She was the one.

All of us have the ability to be the one. All of us have something to contribute to someone else.

The story in the Bible about the feeding of the 5,000 makes this very point.

Jesus noticed the large crowd gathering and asked His disciples about food for all of the people. There wasn't enough money to buy food for everyone. There was only a boy with five loaves and two fish. "But what is that among so many?" asked a disciple. The need was too great. What they had was too small. But the boy gave it to Jesus anyway.

Long before there was a General Motors campaign, that boy was the one. When he gave what he had to God, it was enough for that moment. The focus was not on what he had and how little it was compared to the number of hungry people. The focus for Lucy was not on how many women needed help. The focus for Diane was not how many babies needed touching. The focus was on giving what they had to God. And for those moments, it was enough.

Mattie Graham knows about being the one. She's done it for years, even though she is confined to a retirement center in Orlando, Florida. She battles sometimes with feeling useless and helpless, since she is old and unable to walk. Yet she has a list of friends and relatives, and she writes them notes of encouragement. She can't get out of the center to go shopping, so she collects cards that have been sent to her and the other residents. She erases what others have written in the cards and writes her own message in them.

Someone is always getting a note from Mattie. Every day she is the one to someone who is feeling left out. I was so impressed by her that my son Graham is named for her.

When she is too tired to send these cards, she prays. Even in fatigue she's the one. "Who else will pray for you if I don't?" she says.

Thomas Merton once said that if we think the world is in bad shape now, imagine what it would be like if the people who have committed their lives to prayer stopped praying. We'd have a *real* mess on our hands, he said.

What good is it to "Be the One" when the result is only temporary? Hunger returns. So does the craving for human contact. So does the pain of disease. So does slavery. So does suffering. Lucy could only point out the needs that she could see. After she is gone, there will continue to be needs. Diane could only hold babies for so long. They would crave human touch again. She can't be there for all of them.

What good is it to "Be the One" when the result is only temporary?

And the people on the hillside gathering to listen to Jesus would surely get hungry again. This boy's offer of his lunch did not permanently solve anything. But as Mother Teresa told me, we can't look at the masses and their needs, or we'll never do anything. We can only look at people and what we can offer them. One at a time.

I am under no illusion that the small efforts we make as individuals, or slightly larger efforts like Heart to Heart's medical airlifts, are going to put an end to suffering. But will they help someone for the moment? Yes. Will they provide hope to a hopeless world? Most definitely. Will these efforts give our own lives purpose, meaning, and significance? No question about it.

Go Now

The command is not "Fix everything." It is "Go now" with whatever you have.

After the devastation caused by Hurricane Andrew in Florida, Heart to Heart organized a shipment of food, toys, and supplies for the victims. Grocery stores donated canned goods, pharmaceutical companies donated medicine, and manufacturers donated toys. Even the railroad companies donated space and shipped more than 1 million pounds of materials to the relief center in Florida.

Several months later I was in Washington, D.C., for a meeting with directors of different relief agencies, and the person in charge of distributing supplies to the victims of Hurricane Andrew singled us out for our efforts. He said many times a truck or a railcar would come in with donated items, and it looked as if a whole city had decided to throw its garage sale leftovers in the truck. Someone had to go through each item and determine if it was usable. He hated to admit this, but much of it went to a landfill along with debris caused by the hurricane.

"We got winter coats, snowsuits, even some skis," he said. "We appreciated the gesture, but we couldn't use a lot of it."

The Heart to Heart shipment was different, he said, because it was on pallets that could be removed by forklifts, in clearly marked boxes that identified the contents. (We've learned something after doing this for a while.)

But what meant so much to this relief director was not that we were organized. It was that every box had a personal note written with a packing marker, by whoever had sealed the box. Some of the boxes said, "We love you," or "Hold your head up," or "We're praying for you," or "Don't give up."

Some of the boxes said, "We love you," or "Hold your head up," or "We're praying for you," or "Don't give up."

Heart to Heart volunteers, who worked through the night packing these boxes and loading them onto pallets in our Kansas City warehouse, didn't want to just send boxes. They wanted to send a message: hope. There's no policy that says to do that. I didn't tell them to. They found the markers. They used what was in their hands. They were the ones.

"It was as if members of our family that we hadn't met were reaching out to us," he said, tearfully, as he described this to the group in Washington. "It wasn't the product—it was the contact." It was the hope.

I have witnessed this kind of meaning in a personal, and even more unexpected, way.

Heart to Heart also shipped items donated by Hallmark— gifts, toys, stuffed animals—to Orlando as part of that city's Re- store Orlando program. At Christmastime people in this pro- gram sponsor a special Christmas Eve picnic and give presents like these donated items to the adults and children.

My mom had been sick with breast cancer for a number of months, and it looked as though she was not going to make it through her next stay in the hospital. I flew to Orlando to be with her and my dad for what appeared to be my last contact with her before she died.

While my dad and I talked softly with her in the hospital room, she had a visitor. He wasn't one of Mom's typical visi- tors. He was one of the homeless people my parents cared for. In recent months he had been in their home, eaten their food, and witnessed hope for his own life. Now, hearing that Mom was sick, he wanted to pay her a visit.

"I brought you something," he said as he approached her. It was a stuffed animal—a little rabbit. It looked odd in the hands of this shabbily dressed grown man.

Before my mom could respond, my dad stood up.

"Gary, let's step into the hall," he said quickly.

We left the man in the room with my mom.

"Did you see what he had in his hand?" my dad asked.

"Yes—a stuffed animal. It's a beautiful gesture," I replied.

"No," my dad said. "Did you *see it?*"

I went back into the room to get a closer look. It was now on the bed next to my nearly unconscious mother.

And I recognized it. The bunny was one of the toys we had shipped to Orlando for the Christmas project several months before. It had been given to this man as a token of comfort from a stranger. Now he was passing it on to someone else who needed comfort.

I returned to the hall, where my dad was blinking back tears.

"Does he know where that rabbit came from?" I asked.

He didn't. He had never heard of Heart to Heart. Didn't

know what I did—only that I was a son visiting from out of town.

He was the one that night in that hospital, just days before my mom died.

Lucy? You have eyes and a voice. Use them to "Be the One."

Diane? You're "only a mother." Use that to "Be the One."

Young boy with the loaves and fish? You have a little food. Use it to "Be the One."

Mattie? Just some greeting cards? Use them to "Be the One."

Homeless man? One of your few possessions is a stuffed bunny rabbit. Using it for someone else makes you the one.

And you? Feeling small? What's that in your hand?

6

THE WHITE ZONE

HEADING FOR THE EDGE OF THE PATH, THE WOMAN knows her destination, even though her head looks straight down at the ground underneath. She is about 30 feet from a white stripe, and there is no question that she is going for it directly. You or I could cover that 30 feet in just a few seconds. That's because most of us would walk to the line.

She can't, though. She has to crawl. Inching, painful movements, like a snail without its protective shell. Those who can walk slowly move around her. No one bends to help. Few look directly at her. It isn't out of politeness, either. They are preoccupied with their own predicament.

The white line is a boundary of sorts. On the side where the woman crawls there is motion. On the other side there is not. One side has life. The other isn't just deathly still—it is literally death. And she is purposefully moving from one side to the other.

The line is a lime material put there by health agencies as an attempt to keep the diseases in the rotting corpses of one side from infesting the slowly moving bodies on the other. Not much of a boundary, from a medical perspective, but it is an honest attempt.

This woman gets to the line and doesn't hesitate as she crosses it with her last bit of strength. The lime dust leaves a trail from the path to her destination, like a turtle's tail leaves a mark in the sand. She stops next to a stack of corpses covered only with flies, lets her weight down from her hands and knees, and dies.

Farther down the path, a woman walking upright stiffly crosses the line, reaches inside her wraparound clothing, and disengages a baby from her skinny, lifeless breast. She gently places him on a waist-high pile of bodies. His arms and legs are still moving as she backs away and, head down, rejoins the crush on the other side. Sometime today he will stop moving.

This is Zaire, near refugee camps where 700,000 people had to flee their homes in Rwanda because of the brutal civil war. But they were avoiding one kind of massacre and walking into another. Those on one side of the line were on their way to the refugee camps. Those on the other side didn't make it.

Ray Mattix, a former Heart to Heart board member and one of our volunteers, witnessed these actions as he moved from one camp to another. We were in that country to bring medical supplies to the camps, but we could see that the need was far greater than the amount of medicine we brought. One look across the line showed us that.

Once you witness something like this frail woman facing the reality of her death, or the mother who knows that her baby won't survive, you have a choice. You can be filled with despair, conclude it's all fruitless, and pack up to go home. Or you can conclude, "We'd better pick up our pace here and do what we can." We have picked up our pace.

> Once you witness something like this frail woman facing the reality of her death, or the mother who knows that her baby won't survive, you have a choice.

We faced the same choice when we were in Calcutta.

We arrived at an orphanage with a truck full of medicine and supplies. Everything had gone fairly smoothly once we landed, and, despite the heat, our delegation enthusiastically unloaded the truck. We formed a human chain, passing the boxes from people on the truck to people on the sidewalk to people inside the orphanage.

For Lori Ketterling, one of our staffers, there seemed to be a great deal of laughter and excitement about actually delivering the supplies. After almost a year of planning and working out details, she was getting to see the fruit of her labor. The mood of the volunteers was festive, she remembers, as they passed the boxes in to the orphanage.

But while we were working, one of the nuns appeared in the doorway of the orphanage. "Excuse me," she said.

They stopped passing the boxes down the chain and looked around. Two teenage boys were carrying a small casket out of the orphanage, and the human chain was blocking their way. Our delegation made room for them and watched as the boys carried the box down the sidewalk on their way to a morgue.

The extreme of enthusiasm, of life giving, of hope, had crashed head-on into death. "No one really spoke after that, but we worked much more quickly than before," Lori said. "It was as if we all thought, 'Well, we didn't get here in time for that one, but if we hurry, maybe we can save the next one.'"

We feel a sense of urgency. Often I struggle with discouragement when I see circumstances that appear hopeless, but then I look at the needs around us and say, "Does God want us to do something about this?" We can't afford to look at that white line in Zaire, or at a tiny casket being taken out of an orphanage, and say, "It's hopeless." There's not enough time for that.

We could discuss whether we are only perpetuating a dependency on outside sources by the people of Rwanda or Calcutta, and that the issue is one of economic justice, political corruption, and misguided motives by leaders over the centuries. And we could sponsor studies from the greatest universities and think tanks to evaluate and analyze the conditions and solutions.

In the meantime, the line separating the living from the dead keeps getting blurred by people crawling across it and lying down, and little caskets keep getting carried out of orphanages.

We don't need more study. We don't need more committees
or focus groups. We don't need to consider the political ramifi-
cations. We need to listen to God. He's saying, "Go now."

Aspirin and Silvadene

When Bob Simms was on one of our assessment trips to
Russia to determine what supplies the hospitals needed, this urgency was evident in the doctors' faces.

They came to him with tears in their eyes, asking if we
could give them antibiotics. Bob asked to see the pharmacy at
one hospital, and what he saw shocked him.

This was a big hospital—1,100 beds—and the pharmacy
was about the size of a closet. There were two bookshelves in
the room, with about three bottles of medicine. That was it. The
hospital was virtually out of everything.

"There wasn't even a bottle of aspirin in there," Bob said.

Later he visited a hospital just for emergency burn victims.
It was where people were brought from major industrial acci-
dents; it had about 75 beds. The doctors had been trained during the Soviet Union's war with Afghanistan, where thousands
of soldiers were burned by napalm and explosives. The hospital
was at capacity with these emergency industry cases.

The doctors asked about a burn cream called Silvadene. They
were running out and could only get it on the black market at an
outrageous price because there was such a shortage. They said
they needed it right away. Bob could see that they were right.

We called Ed Connolly, who was president of the corporate
foundation for one of the largest pharmaceutical companies in
the world, Hoechst Marion Roussel (now a part of Aventis), the
manufacturer of Silvadene. He saw to it that several pallets of
the cream were ready for the airlift.

Six weeks later we were back at that hospital with a shipment of medicine, and the doctors asked if we remembered to
bring some Silvadene.

Bob had some in his duffel bag right there and said there
were boxes of it downstairs.

"They showed me what they had left—they were down to
the last third of their last jar," he said.

Interestingly, it was while we were planning this airlift to St. Petersburg that we were struck with the urgency of a completely different situation. Hurricane Andrew had just ripped into the coastline of Florida, killing dozens and displacing thousands of people.

We put together a plan and called some Kansas City television stations that were familiar with Heart to Heart from stories they had done about previous airlifts. We told them we needed their help right away to respond to the needs of the people of Florida. They announced on the air that viewers could help the victims of Hurricane Andrew by donating food, bottled water, clothing, and supplies. The donations were needed for a shipment going there in the next few days, the announcers said.

Hurricane Andrew had just ripped into the coastline of Florida, killing dozens and displacing thousands of people.

Food stores agreed to be drop-off points for the donations, and soon all of Kansas City knew that a relief effort for Florida was under way. Traditional lines of competition were erased, as various grocery store chains, and radio and television stations got involved—even telecommunications rivals AT&T and Sprint worked together on this.

Carl Seaton, owner of Seaton United Van Lines, once again allowed us to use his warehouse to store the supplies. But I'm sure he didn't anticipate how the people of Kansas City would respond to the people of Florida. In fact, when he saw how his warehouse had been taken over by all of these donations, he said to me, "Gary, what have you done to my company?"

He meant that in at least two ways. First, he wondered how he could still run his business when his storage space was completely occupied by items that weren't producing revenue for him. Second, though, he saw how his offer to help had created a new excitement and motivation in his employees as they caught

the vision of what it means to make a difference in needy people's lives.

Seaton employees and hundreds of volunteers worked
around the clock, organizing the items, putting them in shipping crates, and stacking them on pallets in the warehouse. Carl
understands that part of his meaning comes from involvement.
He's a "Go now" guy. We set up a dispatch center in his office.
At one point the list of places that had material waiting for pick-
up was 30 feet long.

For a while, it looked as if this enthusiasm had gone to
waste when reports came from Florida that there were no usable roads going into the destruction area. How would we get
these containers to their intended destination?

But once again Carl Seaton came up with the answer.

He put us in contact with Kansas City Southern Railroad,
and they said they would give us as many railcars as we needed. They also said they would transport them to Louisiana and
Florida.

We filled 47 train cars—using volunteer help—with 2 million pounds of food, medicine,
and water, and the shipment
was there in a matter of days after the hurricane.

> We filled
> 47 train cars—
> using volunteer help—
> with 2 million pounds
> of food, medicine,
> and water.

But it didn't stop there. People who saw the needs kept giving. Four weeks after starting
the drive, we saw there was no
letup in the donations and offers
to help. Residents of Kansas
City caught the sense of urgency
and *wanted* to respond. It meant
something to them. It allowed
them to fulfill their purpose.

One of the most unique responses came from Kansas City
firefighters. News reports out of Florida said that, three weeks
after the hurricane, local firefighters still hadn't been able to go
home because of the continuing fires, rescues, and other dan-

gers. They had been working around the clock since the storm
began.

Kansas City firefighters organized a way to give their Florida counterparts some relief by volunteering to work their shifts
in Dade County, while other Kansas City firefighters covered
the shifts of their absent colleagues. Everyone did a little extra
to make it happen and to keep it from costing the Kansas City
workers vacation time. The Florida crews got to go home.

Once the response to Florida victims was under way, we
turned our attention back to hospitals in Russia.

Star Throwing

Of course it is possible to get *too* overwhelmed by the urgency of the needs around us. But I am uncomfortable with the
way people respond to Jesus' statement, "You have the poor
among you always" (Matt. 26:11; Mark 14:7; John 12:8). Often
we use it as an excuse for inaction because we believe the problem isn't fixable. As soon as we help these burn victims in St.
Petersburg, other victims will appear somewhere else. So why
do anything?

Paul Clem, part of our delegation to Calcutta, wondered
about this when he saw how relatively few people we were able
to help in a city with millions more diseased and dying whom
we didn't help. It was obvious, though, that he had been affected by the life of Mother Teresa.

"We could have helped 50,000 people, and as soon as we
left, there would have been 50,000 more," he said. "But that
doesn't absolve me from the responsibility to touch whoever is
within the reach of my hand today."

Albert Schweitzer said, "I have always held firmly to the
thought that each one of us can do a little to bring some portion
of misery to an end." I believe that this is the only way we will
truly be happy.

Loren Eiseley illustrates this in his story *The Star Thrower.*
Eiseley, a naturalist and scientist, tells of walking along the
beach one morning, carefully avoiding what the tide had deposited on the shore overnight. The beach, he wrote, was "littered with the debris of life." Included in that debris were

starfish, so many that it looked as if the sky had showered them down. But Eiseley saw something else as he walked. He saw a boy kneel in the sand, pick up a starfish, inspect it to see if it was still alive, and throw it back into the ocean. It sailed neatly above the waves, landed, then settled under the surface. It would live for at least another day.

The boy continued this for some time.

They had a brief conversation. "Death is the only successful collector," Eiseley told the boy. But the boy kept looking for survivors and sending them back to their homes.

Eiseley watched, full of scientific certainty that the boy's actions were fruitless and for fairy tales. But later, in the emptiness and quiet of his room, he concluded that the star thrower might be onto something after all. "It was as though at some point the supernatural had touched hesitantly, for an instant, upon the natural."

He returned to the beach.

"I picked up a star whose tube feet ventured timidly among my fingers while, like a true star, it cried soundlessly for life," he wrote. "I saw it with an unaccustomed clarity and cast it far out" (pp. 184-85).

Was he able to save all of the starfish that day? No. Even if he did, the next time the tide came in, thousands more would be deposited on the shore and die.

But he responded to what he saw, and helped those within his reach. It may not have mattered to many, but it mattered to a few.

Eiseley hints at something that we don't often talk about when it comes to responding to the needs of other people. The reason he couldn't get away from the idea of saving some starfish is that it wasn't just a matter of saving some starfish. It was a matter of seeing how the supernatural world meets the natural world when we respond to need. It was about participating in something bigger than ourselves.

> *Was he able to save all of the starfish that day? No.*

Martin Buber said that we were created to bring those two worlds—the supernatural and the natural—together. We do that when we see someone in need and respond. Something outside of ourselves occurs when we do. We give hope, and we connect to the broader purpose for our existence. That's what the star thrower was doing. It's what we all can do.

I believe that part of what makes us uniquely human is not only our ability to see and respond to the needs of others but also our inner *need* to do so. Eiseley simply could not avoid it. We can't either if we allow ourselves to be confronted. The sooner we see this, the sooner we engage in something much bigger than ourselves. The poor we *will* always have with us. We won't meet all people's needs. But the question isn't just about them, it's also about *us*.

> I believe that part of what makes us uniquely human is not only our ability to see and respond to the needs of others but also our inner need to do so.

Every one of us wants to find purpose. What is the real meaning of life? On many occasions people came to Jesus to ask this most basic of questions.

The answer was simple, yet profound. Love God with your heart, soul, mind, and strength. And then love your neighbor. Just two things. Love God, love others. Serve God, serve others.

If you took a poll of people who believed in God, I think you would find general agreement that our purpose is found in relationship with Him. However, few would consider the call to serve one another as essential to our happiness and fulfillment, or to our purpose for living. But if we're going to believe these words that are in both the Old and New Testaments of the Bible several times, then we must believe that part of our purpose for living lies in service to others.

My point is this: When we invest ourselves in relieving the

suffering of those around us, we do at least two things. Obviously, we relieve some suffering, but perhaps just as importantly we give our own lives meaning.

I wish I could have rushed to that crawling woman in Zaire as she passed from life to death in the white zone. I would have liked to reach into my medical bag and give her some medicine to cure her disease. I wish I could have rushed to the baby of the woman when she placed him on a stack of corpses, still alive. I would have liked to have picked him up, fed him, bathed him, educated him, and given him a future. I wish I could have gotten to Calcutta a day earlier so that maybe that child wouldn't have been carried out in a casket.

Try as we might, we will not save everyone. Zaire and Calcutta will still be "littered with the debris of life." But it isn't just about saving people from crossing into the white zone. It's also about those of us who are in a white zone of our own, living lives that have no meaning. It's about crossing from that white zone into the land of the living again. The people in Zaire were passing from life to death. I think it's possible for us to pass from death to life. But we don't have to crawl. We just have to notice the line.

Try as we might, we will not save everyone. Zaire and Calcutta will still be "littered with the debris of life."

Bob Simms got the message from burn victims in St. Petersburg. Loren Eiseley got the message from a starfish.

We must act soon. For them and us.

7

HANDLES
ON THE BARN

ONCE THERE WAS A FARMER WHO NEEDED TO MOVE his barn across the field. He called to his neighbors for help, and as all good neighbors would do, they came over. They got on one side of the barn to push, but it started to tip over. They got on the other side to pull, but most of them didn't have a place where they could get a good grip. They tried to circle the building and move together, but only those on the corners had a place for their hands.

Finally, frustrated, they gave up.

The next day the farmer called to his neighbors again.

"My barn still needs moving," he said.

The neighbors were still willing, but less enthusiastic.

"We tried all day yesterday and couldn't budge it," they said. "How will today be different?"

"Come and see," the farmer said.

During the night he had put handles all around the barn. Now the neighbors could put their strength into the task. This time they could move the barn across the field.

I am convinced that the reason many people don't invest part of themselves into the needs of others isn't just selfishness or coldheartedness. I believe that most people really do want to help other people. But the reason many people don't get involved is that they don't know how. They might try a little, just as the neighbors did in this Amish parable, but they experience resistance because they don't know where they could be useful. They don't have any handles.

People watch the news, for instance, and see devastation from earthquakes or wars but don't even think about being part of the relief of the victims' misery because they can't imagine where they would go to get involved. Maybe there is a request for money, or there is a drop-off site for clothes or canned goods, but nothing for them to get *personally* involved in seeing the help reach its destination.

If they knew how to get involved—if they saw handles—I believe they would get involved.

Finding Handles

Mike Meyers, a Vietnam War veteran I mentioned in chapter 2, understands how handles can lead to involvement. When he went with us on our airlift to Vietnam, it was his first time back since he had been there in combat in 1971 as a door gunner on a Huey helicopter. His memory was of screaming through the jungle, with an 18-year-old pilot flying him at 175 miles per hour 10 feet off the ground, shooting at anything that moved.

He heard about Heart to Heart through news reports, and when he called, we were in the beginning stages of our Vietnam project. He became a significant part of our delegation, and he spoke to several groups while he was there, including the American Chamber of Commerce and a reunion of newspeople who covered the war 20 years before.

What moved him more than meeting with these groups who talked about the past, though, was an encounter he had with a vendor on a street in Hanoi. On his first morning there, he went outside with his video camera and heard someone say "Hello." It was a pedicab driver, and even though he didn't know much English, he wanted to talk. A nearby merchant translated, and they had a brief conversation.

The next morning Mike went outside again, and the pedicab driver was there again, only this time he had his little boy with him, dressed in a suit. On either side of the cab was a new decal—one side was an American flag, the other Canadian. He didn't know where Mike was from, so he wanted to cover at least two English-speaking countries!

Then the driver showed Mike his leg. There were holes in it. The driver said, simply, "American."

But he said it proudly, not accusingly, Mike said. Their veterans admire our veterans, as though they had all gone through something terrible together. The driver wanted to be friends.

That week Mike took a truckload of medicine and supplies to the main hospital in Da Nang. It had 850 beds with no mattresses or air-conditioning.

"The doctors and nurses couldn't believe we had brought them burn cream," he said. "They kept saying, 'We have so many burn victims' because most people still cook over open fires." When they saw the boxes of surgical instruments—scalpels, scissors, forceps, and so on—it was as if we were giving them the most precious thing they had ever seen.

> Then the driver showed Mike his leg. There were holes in it.

The Vietnamese, like most people, value a gift more highly when it is brought to them personally by the giver. Doctors who treated victims from both sides of the war repeatedly shook Mike's hand and hugged him with gratitude.

One doctor in particular, Dr. Le Ngoc Dung, had been instrumental in saving American lives during the Tet offensive. He showed Mike his photo album of patients, which went back as far as the war years. There were several photos of Dr. Le treating U.S. soldiers' wounds. He estimated that he attended to more than 175 U.S. soldiers' head wounds alone during that particularly vicious part of the war.

When the U.S. troops evacuated South Vietnam, Dr. Le was viewed by the Communists as an intellectual threat. He was put in a Communist "reeducation" facility, which was essentially a prison camp. The tasks given to Dr. Le and his fellow prisoners were to find and clear land mines and to rebuild the rail system for the railroad.

That didn't seem like a very good use of Dr. Le's neurosurgical skills. His fellow prisoners came to the same conclusion. If a mine blew up and injured them, they wanted Dr. Le to be available. So they protected him by keeping him back from the front lines.

Eventually, word filtered through the ranks that this Dr. Le was the same one who saved the lives of many North Vietnamese officers during the war. Those officers eventually got him out of the camp and put him where he was most useful—in the Da Nang hospital, which treats nearly 40,000 patients per year.

As Mike toured this hospital with Dr. Le he was taken back by the outdated equipment and shortage of supplies.

One of Dr. Le's photo albums showed him at work within recent months, treating tumors. Some of these tumors were the size of softballs. Mike asked to see the instruments Dr. Le was using. They were tools given to him by American doctors 25 years ago.

If Dr. Le needed to remove a brain tumor, for instance, he used a hand-powered drill to get into the skull—a procedure that takes three hours before he even gets to the tumor. He knew there were better instruments. The electric equivalent in the United States takes 20 minutes to reach the tumor. He also showed Mike a brochure of what he *really* wanted—a special neurosurgical instrument that would break up the tumor and remove it by water vibration and suction. The price in the brochure was $120,000.

As soon as Mike got back to the United States, he didn't wait for another Heart to Heart project before he did something for someone else. He started looking for one of those instruments for Dr. Le.

After he had been involved in meeting needs in Vietnam, he saw that he could continue on his own—the handles were there. He grabbed on, and the barn began moving.

He called around to hospitals and manufacturers and found a used instrument, exactly like the one Dr. Le showed him in the brochure. The price was $30,000. A few calls to some foundations put him in touch with a company that not only bought the machine for Dr. Le but also donated an electronic scalpel instrument that cauterizes during incision, and paid for the shipping.

The story gets better. Through Mike's contacts, Dr. Le was able to come to the U.S. for some additional training, and Mike introduced him to the administration of Rockhurst College in Kansas City. Out of that meeting developed an exchange program where students from Rockhurst can go to Vietnam and work with Dr. Le—and his new equipment—in the Da Nang hospital. Vietnamese doctors will be able to come to Kansas City and work there.

Mike visited Vietnam a second time. "I think I can finally have a positive impact on them by getting medicine and surgical equipment there. It's better than flying over their country and shooting at them," he told me. "It's like a light went on in my head."

Or he'd found a handle.

That's what happened with Gary Bugg, a former hospital administrator and chief executive officer of a health maintenance organization. He had gone with us on an airlift to Russia. As someone directly involved in health care in the U.S., he wanted to see how health care was being practiced since the fall of the Soviet Union.

He couldn't believe what he saw. There was such an excess of doctors that their salaries were about $10 per month—cabdrivers and beggars made more than that. But there was a shortage of everything else. Disposable instruments were reused hundreds of times. Needles were tossed into a bowl of disinfectant for a moment, then reattached to syringes and used over and over. The shortage of anesthetics was so great that he saw some gruesome operations occur without any anesthetic at all.

In one operation a surgeon's assistant kept track of the patient's pulse by holding the wrist and looking at her watch.

In one operation a surgeon's assistant kept track of the patient's pulse by holding the wrist and looking at her watch. When the pulse would race, the assistant would nod, and the surgeon would give a little more painkiller.

So when he came back to the U.S., Gary had a different perspective on the needs of others. He had a chance to put that perspective into action a short time later.

The day we were scheduled to leave for our airlift to Vietnam, a bomb exploded outside the Murrah Federal Building in Oklahoma City. It was one of the worst terrorist acts in U.S. history. We grieved over it as we prepared to leave the country, but knew we had to continue with our plan. Gary had a different idea.

He called me just minutes before I left my house for the airport—hours after the explosion—and said, "We have to do something for these people in Oklahoma City." I understood his concern and also wanted to do something, but I needed to get going to the airport. I was pretty blunt with him. "Whatever you want to do, you're going to have to do it," I told him.

Actually, that's a pretty good philosophy in general when it comes to relieving suffering. "Go now."

Gary went. He called local stores and hospitals. He called the news media, and announcers told their audiences of Gary's idea to help. Within the day he had enough surgical masks, back supports, respirators, diapers, and food to fill two semitrailers. He went to the manager of the local Dillons store, who went to his truck drivers and said, "Who wants to drive to Oklahoma City right now?" Drivers volunteered. Dillons supplied the trucks, loaded them, then unloaded them in Oklahoma at no charge. The Kansas Turnpike authorities gave the trucks a free pass. Police officers removed barricades and allowed the trucks to get right to the victims.

All of this occurred the day of the bombing. Most of Heart to Heart was over an ocean somewhere, unavailable to give Gary advice or help.

Is Gary Bugg a Superman? No. Gary found a handle.

"I would have never attempted such a thing had I not witnessed those scenes in Russia," he said. "I would have never presumed I was capable of this."

All he did was call people and tell them what was needed.

"When someone tells us what we can do, we respond," he said.

Had Gary said, "Let's put together a task force, study the situation, see what our resources are, and check our calendars," they would still have been meeting by the time we returned from Vietnam.

"If you sit around and think about it, you can talk yourself out of it," he said. "But this is about getting out of yourself and considering others. It's contagious."

Gary was only half-kidding when he speculated to me that there must be a chemical response—a release of endorphins—in human beings when they help someone. It makes them want to help again and again, he said.

"After Russia I knew that I was incapable of turning my head away when I saw someone in need," Gary said. "If I see it or hear about it, I have to respond. All of the people who helped with the Oklahoma City relief are now in the same position."

> *"After Russia I knew that I was incapable of turning my head away when I saw someone in need."*

Personally, I don't think it's chemical. It's not endorphins. It's purpose. When people see that being involved in the needs of others is part of their purpose for existing, they can't forget it. They find the handle.

Nishan Kazazian, a Los Angeles dentist, spends part of every year doing dental work on victims of earthquakes and war in Armenia. Heart to Heart has worked with him and other dentists in that part of the world, and I am impressed by his approach to his own success on the West Coast. He likens it to the parable about a man who went away and left considerable money in the hands of his servants. "To one he gave five bags of gold, to another two, to another one" (Matt. 25:15).

When the man came home, the servant with five bags

showed that he had invested the money and had made five more, and the man was pleased. The servant with two invested his and showed that he had made two more, and the man was also pleased. The servant with one had buried the bag and gave it back to the man exactly as he had received it. This angered the man, and he punished that servant for being lazy.

"Where much is given, much is expected," Nishan said. "I don't believe I was given this successful dental practice so I could have a big house and car."

Nishan found purpose in his success—not to use it all on himself, but to see it as a gift that can be given to others.

"I sleep less and work harder when I am in Armenia, but I come back stronger and more energized than I would if I had gone to an exotic vacation villa," he said. He is energized in part by his sense of meaning and significance, and in part by the response he gets from those he helps.

"They bring me flowers from their gardens," he said. "They don't have anything else, so I know they are gifts from their hearts. That gives me more joy than any vacation I can imagine."

Nishan has a handle. He knows how to get the barn moving.

But people don't have to go to Oklahoma City, Vietnam, or Armenia to find purpose and meaning. The handles are all around us. Eunice Powell, a woman who retired years ago, volunteers her time in our office to stuff envelopes, answer phones, and do whatever she can to help. She's not able to go on the big international airlifts, but she has found her handle right in our office.

> All people
> can do something,
> right where they are,
> with what they
> have, right now.

All people can do something, right where they are, with what they have, right now. And when they understand the need and are given a handle to grab, people respond. I like Rabbi Harold Kushner's response to the Oklahoma

City tragedy. Someone asked him how he could believe in God when tragedies like that occur. He said that it made him even stronger in his belief in God, because he saw the thousands of people reach out to these victims, even though they were total strangers. Bad things happen. Good people respond.

Counting the Cost

Henri Nouwen tells the story of an old man who meditated every morning under a large tree on the bank of a river in India. He opened his eyes after meditating one morning and saw a scorpion caught in the fast current of the river. The current pulled the scorpion close to the roots of the tree where the man was sitting, and it became frantic as it struggled in the web of roots and the current.

The old man immediately stretched himself onto the roots and reached for the drowning scorpion. But as soon as he touched it, the scorpion instinctively swung its tail and stung the man. The man jumped back, then regained his balance on the roots and again stretched to save the creature. The tail snapped and stung the man repeatedly, until his hands were swollen from the poison and his face distorted by pain.

At that moment a passerby saw the old man on the roots, struggling with the scorpion, and shouted, "Hey, stupid old man. What's wrong with you? Only a fool risks his life for the sake of an ugly, useless creature. Don't you know that you may kill yourself to save that ungrateful animal?"

The old man calmly replied, "Friend, because is it the nature of the scorpion to sting, why should I give up my own nature to save?" (*Seeds of Hope*, 124-25).

I have observed a lot of people who say that before they get involved in the needs of others, they want to wait until they see if this is what they *should* do. They count the cost and consider if the involvement will "sting" like the scorpion. Very few of them ever move outside of that world of introspection. But if those same people come face-to-face with someone else in need and see how they can help, they stop their introspection and respond. It's our nature. It's how we're made.

There is something else I have observed after seeing people

discover handles for their own compassion. Once they see how needy the world really is, and how important and rewarding it is to respond to those needs, they have a newfound confidence in using their own abilities and talents. Or, as one volunteer told me, "Once you've seen a village full of people dying from leprosy, nothing is too hard to do."

Mike Meyers's abilities are in comprehending and evaluating complex situations. He is a manager for international trade contracts. He oversees projects that cross several countries, businesses, and governments. Before that he was a commodities trader. Now he has another outlet for those talents: finding ways to ease the suffering of people. He can comprehend, evaluate, and respond to needy people in the same way he does in his business.

He has even started his own nonprofit company with Mark Schlansky of McDonnell Douglas, who also was with Heart to Heart in Vietnam. The company procures and distributes medical equipment to hospitals and clinics in that country. The two maintain their regular jobs while giving a good deal of their spare time to ministry: finding ways to relieve suffering.

There can be a danger in all of this. Everyone knows someone who has gotten so involved in the needs of others that he or she has gone off the deep end and shirked personal or family responsibilities to the point of self-destruction. One of our volunteers was so taken with the suffering that he witnessed in Russia that, weeks after he had returned to his home in Illinois, it was still all he could think about.

He remembers sitting on his back patio, wondering how some of the patients were whom he visited in the hospital, when his teenage daughter joined him.

"Dad, we need you to come all the way home now," she said. "We need you here."

Action and Contemplation

Malcolm Muggeridge, the great British writer who wrote about Mother Teresa in his book *Something Beautiful for God,* tells of an incident that shows the difference between his response to seeing the needs of people in Calcutta and the response of Mother Teresa.

As Muggeridge's driver was trying to negotiate the car through the packed streets of Calcutta, the unthinkable happened: The driver knocked down a pedestrian. The driver jumped out, grabbed the injured man, put him in the seat beside him, and drove away at top speed to the nearest hospital.

The hospital, Muggeridge described, "was a scene of inconceivable confusion and horror, with patients stretched out on the floor, in the corridors, everywhere. While I was waiting, a man was brought in who had just cut his throat from ear to ear. It was too much; I made off, back to my comfortable flat and a stiff whisky and soda."

Muggeridge said that the difference between himself and Mother Teresa was easy to see: "I ran away and stayed away; Mother Teresa moved in and stayed" (pp. 17-18).

Personally, I think Muggeridge's flight is not the response most of us would make. Neither is Mother Teresa's. But I believe that once people see this kind of suffering, they will look for ways to help someone regardless of where they end up. As long as they have handles.

My daughter Amy went with us on our airlift to Calcutta, and she worked in the Home for Dying Destitutes. She talked about it so much when she got back to college that it awakened a desire among other women in her dormitory to do something similar. One year later she organized her own group to go back there. She never once asked for my help! Most of the group came from middle-class, middle-American homes. But they saw that it was possible to get out of themselves and focus on the needs of someone else. It was attractive. And they had a handle.

We can't be constantly active, and we can't respond to every need that we see.

There is at least one other danger involved in this view of finding our true purpose. The danger is that we may concentrate so much on what we should *do* that we lose sight of what we should *be*. We can't be constantly active, and we can't respond to every need that we see. In the case of Mother Teresa when she saw the dying woman in the street, she didn't need to stop and ponder what to do. She picked up the woman. When Gary Bugg heard about the Oklahoma City bombing, he didn't wonder if he should do something. He just responded.

But human beings can't constantly do things. As one preacher said, "We are human *beings*, not human *doings*." Getting away to a quiet place regularly is just as important as grabbing the next handle on the barn. It helps clarify what our role can be in relieving suffering. It helps clarify which handles we should grab.

Henri Nouwen writes, "In the heart of much involvement there are words of withdrawal. In the midst of action there is contemplation. And after much togetherness there is solitude" (*Out of Solitude*, 13).

After His baptism and before His life of ministry as an adult, Jesus went to the desert, alone. Before He fed the multitude, He went to a "lonely place" with His disciples (Mark 6:32). Before His trial with Pilate, He went alone to Gethsemane.

He wouldn't do one without the other, and neither should we. In his book *Silence on Fire*, William Shannon writes: "A crude way of putting it would be to say that I spent so much time doing the things that would please God that I had no time left just to be with God" (p. 16).

Mother Teresa and the Missionaries of Charity have mass every morning before they begin their day's tasks. "Prayer enlarges the heart until it is capable of containing God's gift of Himself," she said (Muggeridge, *Something Beautiful for God*, 47). That gift then is lived out during the day as they respond to people in need.

The handles are there. You only need to grab onto the one that's nearby. Once you do, you'll see that the barn is covered with them.

8

FROM HEAD TO HEART

FR. GENE ARTHUR HAD SEEN PAIN BEFORE, BUT NOT like this. During the Vietnam War he was a chaplain at Fort Riley, Kansas, and he faced a countless number of severely wounded soldiers as they came back from battle. He would pray for them, minister to them, and encourage them, all in an effort to keep them alive.

When he went to Vietnam as part of our delegation, though, 20 years after the war ended, he saw something he had never seen in all of his life as a priest and minister. He had never seen people thrown away to die.

He was describing the leprosy village we visited.

Squalor is the word that fits best.

I described the village leader in chapter 4. His age was indeterminable because of how sick he was; he had suffered a stroke and was in a hospital. But when he heard that we were bringing medicine and food to his village, he wanted to see it happen. Then, when he heard that there was a priest among us, he asked for a blessing.

We went to the leader's hut, made of mud and dirt, and a few of us could fit inside. He was paralyzed on one side, partially devoured by leprosy, and overcome with weakness. Father Arthur gripped the man's hand strongly and gave him a traditional Catholic blessing, saying, "May God come to you and strengthen you. May God come to you and bless your work."

The blessing may have been traditional, but the result was not.

The priest had a personal revelation.

"It was God telling me, 'I brought you here for a purpose—to minister to this person, in this moment, now,'" he said.

These were the rejects of the world. Yet Father Arthur said God made it clear that He brought him halfway around the world for that very moment, that very person.

"I am not an emotional man, but this was like being hit with a two-by-four, and my tears flowed freely."

What happened to Father Arthur has happened to all of those who have seriously confronted the words in Matt. 25. It says that eventually all people will be confronted with the question of whether they treated God and others properly. It's a familiar section of Scripture: "For when I was hungry, you gave me food; when thirsty, you gave me drink; when I was a stranger you took me into your home, when naked you clothed me; when I was ill you came to my help, when in prison you visited me" (vv. 35-36).

Whatever you have done to these people—the hungry, thirsty, homeless, naked, sick, and imprisoned—you have done to God. That's what verse 40 says.

That same section says that some people will complain and say, in sum, "How were we supposed to know that it was You, God? Had we known it was You, we would have treated You differently!"

But God has already let us know that it is himself in these hungry, thirsty, alien, naked, sick, and imprisoned people.

Tony Campolo, a sociologist, writer, and speaker, says that Christians in general tend to focus more of their attention on less-important matters than those Jesus raises here.

"What will you tell Jesus when He says, 'When I was hungry, did you feed me?' Are you going to say, 'No, Jesus, but I didn't smoke'? And when He says, 'Did you take care of me when I was sick?' Will you say, 'No, but I didn't play the Lottery'?"

Campolo also addresses the reluctance to provide for people based on their appearance. In his book *Is Jesus a Republican or a Democrat?* Campolo says that, when God asks him if he provided for the needy, "I do not think it will wash if I say, 'I thought about it, but they did not look trustworthy.' The Lord just might answer such an excuse by saying, 'You should have done what I asked you to do. In turn, I would have held them responsible for what they did with the money'" (p. 160).

And even though Gene Arthur has been a priest for all of his adult life, those verses have only recently come alive for him.

"I knew in my head that these verses meant that we love Jesus by loving these people, but until this experience I didn't know it in my heart," he said. "During my prayer with the village leader, it moved from my head to my heart."

This is a difficult and emotionally charged subject. Especially when you witness just how needy some people are, and then imagine that how you respond to them is how you respond to God. Frankly, I don't always know how to respond to things I see or hear about.

For instance, Michael Pitts, who was with us in Calcutta at the Home for Dying Destitutes, *thought* he had seen the neediest of the needy while he was working with the dying men in that house. But at the end of the day he and another volunteer witnessed something that makes me shudder. In that home there are four rows, each with 10 cots; each cot is occupied by someone dying; each person dying is also afflicted with some form of dysentery. One of Michael's tasks was to carry bedpans from the men to a back room, put them in a stack, and bring clean ones back to them.

Michael assumed that life couldn't get any lower than it was for these men. He changed his mind when he and the other volunteer carried out the garbage from the home at the end of the day. Remember, this is garbage from a houseful of diseased, dying people. The volunteers dragged two garbage cans out the back door of the house, walked for a block, then turned the

> What a discovery—
>
> to find that there are
>
> people living even lower
>
> than those in the
>
> Home for Dying Destitutes.

corner to reach the neighborhood open-air dump. They emptied one, set it down, and picked up the other.

Apparently they hadn't completely emptied the first one

because, before they had set the second one down, a woman was picking through what was still in the first. They waited until she was done, then carried both empty cans back to the home. Before he turned the corner, though, Michael looked back. Several more people had appeared and were sifting through what the men had just poured out.

"What do you look for in *this* garbage?" he asked.

What a discovery—to find that there are people living even lower than those in the Home for Dying Destitutes. Juxtapose that with a statement that says how we treat them is how we treat God. That's complicated, but Father Arthur understood it when he gripped the hand of the village chief.

Factoring the Poor into Your Life

Another one of our volunteers to Calcutta came to a similar conclusion, but instead of responding to the needs of Calcutta—a concept he found overwhelming—he now responds to the needs of the people near his own office in Missouri. Fred Hahn is an ear, nose, and throat doctor, and there are specific images that stand out in his mind that motivate him to do something for someone within his everyday reach.

One, as has been the case for so many of us, comes from the Home for Dying Destitutes. He remembers one man who was in his 40s, emaciated, stretched out flat on his cot, except for his arm. That arm held up a Leon Uris paperback book to read. The man had been an English teacher in Tibet but now had untreatable diarrhea and was slowly dying.

"In the U.S. he would have had a stool culture where we could identify the parasite, give him some medicine, and send him back to teaching," Fred said. "People who typically would have a long life face death prematurely."

That image captured his attention because it helped him realize that, in some cases, these were educated people like himself. He hadn't seen this in such a stark way before. And they couldn't do anything to keep their physical needs from killing them.

The other image that stands out for Fred Hahn is what he saw as he walked on the sidewalk of Calcutta toward the Kali temple. He saw a woman in her 20s, lying against a wall on the sidewalk. The baby lying next to her struggled silently, trying to nurse, but could not.

"He was trying desperately to hang on to life, and his mother was too weak to help him," he said.

These images got Fred to thinking about what it means to provide health care to the poor who live in his city in the U.S. Now he spends part of his workweek at a clinic in his county's general hospital, providing services for patients who can't pay.

"That lady with the baby brought a sense of urgency out of me," he said. "It made me think that, as an individual, there is something I can do. And that it is sacred."

Father Arthur and Fred Hahn experienced a reality that several of us have found as we have consciously decided that we have a responsibility to those less fortunate than us. Bob Simms, one of our volunteers to Russia, said that when we are involved like this, everything is right for that moment. "It's a small window that allows us to be in the real world, however briefly," he said. "People just know that this is how things are supposed to be."

That responsibility wasn't first spoken of in Matt. 25, though. In the second and third books of the Bible, God's declaration of our responsibility to the needy is clear: Do not oppress the homeless (see Exod. 23:8). The second is specific even about our *providing* for them. When you harvest your crops, don't harvest all the way to the edges, it says. Don't pick your fields clean or pick up what drops. "You shall leave them for the poor and the alien" (Lev. 19:9-10).

In other words, we will have plenty for ourselves and for what we will sell *and* for those who don't have anything. Factor the poor into your life, it says. Help those who are at the mercy of the social and economic system, it says. This is what the pharmaceutical company Hoechst Marion Roussel now does with the burn cream Silvadene. Once company officials saw how badly it was needed in the Newly Independent States, Vietnam, and elsewhere, they began manufacturing more than the market called for so they would have enough to give Heart to Heart for our airlifts. That is a modern-day fulfillment of the responsibility we have for those who can't always fend for themselves.

This is not a new concept. In his book *Soul of Politics,* Jim Wallis tells of an experiment he and some others conducted. They looked up every reference to the poor and oppressed in the Bible and saw that only the topic of idolatry was mentioned more often. One person took this experiment a dramatic step farther. He took a pair of scissors and cut out each of those references. When he came to statements like the one in Isa. 58:6-7, "Is not this the fast that I choose . . . to share your bread with the hungry, and bring the homeless poor into your house; when you see the naked, to cover them, and not to hide yourself from your own kin?" (NRSV), he cut those verses out. And thousands more that were similar.

When he was done, the Bible was held together by threads.

If you believe the message of the Bible, as I do, then we have to confront our response to those who are less fortunate than us.

This is how Mother Teresa explained it in her interview with Malcolm Muggeridge in *Something Beautiful for God.*

MOTHER TERESA: Love and faith go together. They complete each other.

MUGGERIDGE: How do you help people find the way of faith and love?

MOTHER TERESA: By getting them in touch with the people, for in the people they will find God.

MUGGERIDGE: You mean that the road to faith and the road to God is via our fellow human beings?

MOTHER TERESA: Because we cannot see Christ we cannot express our love to him; but our neighbors we can always see, and we can do to them what if we saw him we would like to do to Christ.

MUGGERIDGE: Isn't it a danger that we may become only social workers or just do the work for the sake of the work?

MOTHER TERESA: It is a danger if we forget to whom we are doing it. . . .

MUGGERIDGE: What you do is to make one see that the

lepers, these children off the street, the destitute, are not just to be pitied; they are marvelous people. How do you do this?

MOTHER TERESA: That's just what a Hindu gentleman said: that they and we are doing social work. But the difference between them and us is that they were doing it for something and we were doing it to somebody (112-14).

* * *

When we consider that we are *supposed* to look out for the needy, because this is also how we treat God, then how we treat others in everyday life takes on a completely different dimension. And the rest of the world notices.

A Different Drum

In his book *The Different Drum,* Scott Peck tells this story about a monastery that had fallen upon hard times. Secularism had taken its toll on this once great order, and the group was down to one decaying house with only five monks left. The abbot and four others were all more than 70 years old. The end of the order was in sight.

In the woods surrounding the monastery there was a little hut that was occasionally used by a rabbi from a nearby town. When he visited, the monks would whisper among themselves, "The rabbi is in the woods. The rabbi is in the woods again."

During one of those visits, it occurred to the abbot that the rabbi could perhaps offer some advice or encouragement as to the remaining monks. Perhaps the rabbi would know or could say something that would save the order.

The rabbi welcomed the abbot at his hut, but when the abbot explained the purpose for his visit, the rabbi could only commiserate with him. "I know how it is," he lamented. "The spirit has gone out of the people. It is the same in my town. Almost no one comes to the synagogue anymore."

So the old abbot and the old rabbi wept together. Then they read part of the Torah and quietly spoke of deep things. The time came when the abbot had to leave. They embraced each other, but the abbot felt incomplete. "I have failed in my purpose for coming here. Is there nothing you can tell me, no piece of advice you can give me that would help me save my dying order?"

"No, I am sorry," the rabbi responded. "I have no advice to give. The only thing I can tell you is that the Messiah is one of you."

When the abbot returned to the monastery, his fellow monks gathered around him and asked, "Well, what did the rabbi say?"

"He couldn't help," the abbot answered. "We just wept and read the Torah together. The only thing he did say, just as I was leaving—it was something cryptic—was that the Messiah is one of us. I don't know what he meant."

In the days and weeks and months that followed, the old monks pondered this and wondered whether there was any possible significance to the rabbi's words. The Messiah is one of us? they thought. If that's the case, who? The abbot? Yes, probably Father Abbot. After all, he has been the leader for more than a generation.

On the other hand, he might have meant Brother Thomas. Certainly Brother Thomas is a holy man. Everyone knows that Thomas is a man of light. Certainly he could not have meant Brother Elred! Elred gets crotchety at times. But when you think about it, even though he is a thorn in people's sides, Elred is almost always right. Maybe the rabbi did mean Brother Elred.

As they contemplated in this manner, the old monks began to treat each other with extraordinary respect.

But surely not Brother Phillip. Phillip is so passive, a real nobody. But then, almost mysteriously, he has a gift for somehow always being there when you need him. He just magically appears by your side. Maybe Phillip is the Messiah.

Of course the rabbi didn't mean me. He couldn't possibly have meant me. I'm just an ordinary person. Yet suppose he did? Suppose I am the Messiah? O God, not me. I couldn't be that much for You, could I?

As they contemplated in this manner, the old monks began to treat each other with extraordinary respect on the off chance that one among them might be the Messiah. And on the off, *off* chance that each monk himself might be the Messiah, they began to treat themselves with extraordinary respect.

Because the forest in which the monastery was situated was beautiful, it so happened that people still occasionally came to visit, to picnic on its lawn, to wander along some of its paths, even now and then to go into the dilapidated chapel to meditate. As they did so, without even being conscious of it, they sensed this aura of extraordinary respect that now began to surround the five old monks and seemed to radiate out from them and permeate the atmosphere of the place. There was something strangely attractive, even compelling, about it. Hardly knowing why, they began to come back to the monastery more frequently to picnic, to play, to pray. They began to bring their friends to show them this special place. And their friends brought their friends.

Then it happened that some of the younger men who came to visit the monastery started to talk more and more with the old monks. After a while one asked if he could join them. Then another. And another. So within a few years the monastery had once again become a thriving order and, thanks to the rabbi's gift, a vibrant center of light and spirituality in the area (13-15).

Do You Love Me?

Brennan Manning, a gifted speaker and writer, said that we express our feelings about God in the way we treat each other. That expression "is manifested neither in being chaste, honest, sober and respectable, nor in church-going, Bible-toting and Psalm singing, but in our deep and delicate respect for one another" (*Ragamuffin Gospel*, 121). Jesus, in the Upper Room with His disciples, told them that their future was based on this declaration: "Love one another as I have loved you" (John 13:34, BECK). To Peter, specifically, He said, "Do you love me? . . . Tend my sheep" (21:16, RSV).

There is a marvelous story of the former mayor of New

York City, Fiorello La Guardia, who was in charge of that city during the Great Depression. On a bitterly cold night in January 1935, he showed up at night court in the ward that served the poorest section of the city. He took the place of the judge for a while and found himself presiding over the case of an old woman charged with stealing a loaf of bread. The shopkeeper was pressing charges because he wanted to teach the woman and the rest of the neighborhood a lesson.

But, as the woman explained to the mayor, her husband had deserted her, her daughter was sick, and her grandchildren were hungry. Since the shopkeeper refused to back down, the mayor/judge had no choice but to uphold the law. The verdict was $10.00 or 10 days in jail. The old woman was horrified. She didn't have the money, and if she went to jail, who would look after those at home?

> The old woman was horrified. She didn't have the money, and if she went to jail, who would look after those at home?

The mayor/judge was not finished, though. He reached into his pocket and pulled out $10.00 to pay the fine. "Furthermore," he said, "I am going to fine everyone in the courtroom 50 cents for living in a town where a person has to steal bread so that her grandchildren can eat. Mr. Bailiff, collect the fines and give them to the defendant."

A bewildered old lady was handed $47.50, 50 cents of which was given by the fuming grocery-store owner, while the rest of the money came from criminals, accused, and police officers. The mayor was given a standing ovation! (*Ragamuffin Gospel*, 91-92).

We are not going to solve the problems of global poverty and disease. But it can't be any clearer than the biblical declaration: look out for one another, provide for one another, take care of one another. That is one of the ways we love God. Doing small things with great love.

The greatest example of this kind of living is in the story "The Cobbler's Visitor," by the great Russian writer Leo Tolstoy. The story is about a cobbler who lost his wife and children. His despair was so great that he told a holy man, "I no longer wish to live. I am without hope."

The holy man replied, "Your despair comes because you wish to live for your own happiness. Read the Gospels: there you will see how God would have you live."

After several days of reading, the cobbler heard a voice that said, "Look out into the street tomorrow, for I shall come."

Every time the cobbler looked up from his work the next day, he saw someone who needed assistance. The cobbler saw an old man shoveling snow, resting frequently and shivering. The cobbler invited him into his store for some food and warmth. He also saw a woman freezing with her baby because she had just sold her shawl to buy food. He gave her an old cloak of his.

He saw a feeble woman with a basket of apples to sell, and saw a boy try to steal one. The cobbler intervened in the struggle, paid for the stolen apple, and the boy helped the woman carry her burden.

But the cobbler was disappointed. He had expected to see God, according to the Voice, and hadn't.

That evening the Voice returned and said, "Don't you know me? It is I." And in the shadows of his room he saw the freezing man, the woman with the baby, the old woman and the boy. He opened his Bible and read, "For I was hungry and you gave me food, I was thirsty and you gave me drink, I was a stranger and you welcomed me . . . As you did it to one of the least of these my brethen, you did it to me" (Matt. 25:35, 40, RSV).

I don't pretend to understand the mystery of this idea that when we love others we love God. I simply know that I am different when I do.

"We cannot walk away from the poor," Tony Campolo writes. "We must respond to their needs. God prefers to be among them, and if we want to be close to God, we must be among them, too" (*Republican or Democrat?* 167).

9

TAKE MY WORLD APART

To love you—take my world apart
To need you—I am on my knees
To love you—take my world apart
*To need you—broken on my knees**
—Jars of Clay

Typically Ray Mattix is a bricklayer for residential construction. For a while, though, he laid bricks to build in a wall of personal self-pity. The American dream he had pursued all of his adult life was turning into an illusion.

One of the most important things in his life was that he was an entrepreneur. He owned his own business and was president of the corporation he had formed. He had many employees, lots of equipment, and lucrative out-of-town contracts. He was proud of the fact that he was on his own.

But as so often happens to young, upstart, undercapitalized businesses during recessions, the business climate proved more difficult than he anticipated, and the competition became relentless. He soon found himself comparing his day-to-day successes and failures with those of his peers, explaining away his disappointments to the luck of the draw, hopeful that he would make it up on the next job.

It wasn't long before he experienced some severe reversals and found it necessary to sell much-needed equipment to raise much-needed cash—quickly. Without the proper equipment, it's very difficult to execute a profitable contract. And without these profitable contracts, the outgo quickly exceeds the income. He soon discovered that the only things left of his business were the liabilities.

He even lost the gamble to mortgage his home. His attitude changed from one of positive pursuit of the dream to defensive maneuvering. He couldn't help but look around at other businesses, thinking how it all came down to luck.

He remembers one day in particular, driving down the interstate in his old Chevy truck, recalling the apparent success of one of his contemporaries, and saying out loud to himself and to God, "How lucky can a guy be? That could have been me. No, that *should* have been me. You know that I have worked as hard and am as smart as I know how to be, and somewhere along the line, I seem to recall something about being promised my *just reward*."

Shortly after Ray's business failed, his church embarked on what it called a Work and Witness project. The project was to travel to the mountains of northern Guatemala and build a church for a congregation that was just getting organized. In addition, the group would help a local orphanage. Ray's task, due to his upbringing on a farm, was to help secure some cattle for the orphanage.

"Ever since that visit, the term 'being on your own' has taken on a whole new meaning to me," he said. "Until then, the term was attached to the American dream. I associated it with success, yuppies, determination, and plenty of positive thinking."

He came face-to-face with a new definition for "being on your own."

The children who lived in that orphanage had lost both parents—murdered by guerrilla activity. These children were vividly, intentionally, cruelly, "on their own."

One building on the orphanage compound caught Ray's eye because it stood farther away from the rest, closer to the main road. Inside were a few chairs, a bed frame, and a table. It clearly had not been used in some time.

"Why isn't this building put to some better use?" Ray asked.

The missionary with him took Ray to the side of the building facing the road. The wall was covered with bullet holes.

"Bullets?" Ray said. "Are you sure it's even safe for us to be here?"

"We'll be out of here by dark," the missionary said. "The guerrillas aren't *completely* cold-blooded.

"In fact," the missionary continued, "they bring little children here themselves under the cover of darkness after they have murdered their parents.

"They're not unreasonable. They wouldn't kill kids on purpose. They just want to be kept on the forefront of everyone's mind."

On the way back down the mountain, Ray and the missionary pulled the car off the coastal highway to watch the ocean. It was getting dark, but they were far enough away from the jungle and felt safe. Looking up, Ray could see a full moon over the water. From his high perch on that black coral shoreline, he saw the ocean rush to the shore, then change its mind and rush back out again.

He thought of the local people there in Santo Domingo; he thought of the missionaries and their daily sacrifices, their pain of loneliness and separation from their family members. He thought of the lifestyle they didn't have.

And then Ray thought of Ramondo, a little boy he had seen at the orphanage earlier that day.

Ray pictured the row of neatly driven nails in one of the shelters, on which hung 44 little toothbrushes. And he pictured Ramondo, standing by his place, looking at Ray—the American with the shiny boots and the clean shirt.

"His little black eyes penetrated mine," Ray said. "Those eyes asked a hundred questions. I hoped they expected no answers."

Ramondo's gaze into Ray was able to do what all the years of the now false and faded security of entrepreneurship were unable to do. All the dealings with bankers, businesspeople, and IRS agents couldn't do what Ramondo did.

"The memory of that little 35-pound kid was able to reach into a soul and pull forth humility from a 200-pound man," Ray said.

God didn't need to use sophisticated language to reach Ray. He merely reminded Ray of his own words, "God, how lucky can a guy be?"

Ray's world had come apart. And Ramondo was part of the rebuilding.

Since then, Ray has gone on several other trips like this and is one of the original members of the Heart to Heart Board of Directors. His American dream has been replaced with a global dream, which is to be an instrument of hope to a needy world.

The Center of the Wheel

At Heart to Heart we have seen that, for many people, an experience with the world's poor and needy is life-changing. It's even more life-changing when you are needy yourself, as in the case of Ray Mattix. Another good example is our procurement coordinator, Barb Nielson, who is a recovering alcoholic.

Barb's first time out of the United States was when she went with us on an airlift to Kyrgyzstan, one of the states created after the fall of the Soviet Union.

"I had visited the pit of hell in my alcoholism," she said, "and everything I did was an attempt to cover the ugliness of my life. I feel as if I was given a gift by going on a trip like this—a gift I didn't deserve. The gift was the freedom to dwell on something other than me."

We see that the world is bigger and needier than we could have ever imagined.

One of the reasons our world is taken apart when we get involved in the needs of others is that it changes our idea that the world revolves around our own personal needs. Instead of thinking we are in the center of the wheel, we see that we are really part of the rim with everyone else. And we see that the world is bigger and needier than we could have ever imagined.

For Jim Kerr, a pharmacist, the world used to be about as big as his hometown.

"Olathe, Kansas, was as big as my picture got," he said. "My life, my job, and my church were all in Olathe, so I had no need to look beyond that."

But when he got involved in our first airlift to Russia, his known world started to bulge at the seams.

"The Russia trip changed my vision and my faith," he said. "And as I look back on it, I wonder if I had either."

As a businessperson, Jim's approach to any venture was to demand to see where the financing was coming from, when the project would start, and when it would finish. He needed things in concrete terms.

"I was in charge of filling a cargo plane," Jim said. "I was in way over my head because I had no idea what I was doing."

But that's what was so right about this experience for Jim. He was living outside his comfort zone. He couldn't control all of the pieces. He had to believe in the vision of the project, and he had to have faith. The plane got filled, the hospitals got their medicines, and Jim's world got taken apart.

He was living outside his comfort zone. He couldn't control all of the pieces.

"Now I ask, 'Is there anything God can't do?'" Jim said.

A few years later he brought his 14-year-old daughter with him on the airlift to Calcutta.

"I didn't want her to have to wait until she was an adult, set in her ways like me, for her world to be taken apart," he said. She saw Sikhs, Hindus, Muslims, and others who don't believe what she believes.

"And she saw that God created *all* of us and uses *all* of us," Jim said. "In my town we tend to think that other people and cultures aren't significant and don't have an impact on the world. My daughter saw that that couldn't be farther from the truth. She saw that God created more than a billion Chinese and Indians. That has broad implications that she didn't consider before."

Something else was taken apart in Jim's life—his understanding of the Bible. "When we were in Calcutta, Mother Teresa said something that has stayed with me," he said. "She said that when Jesus said in Matt. 25 that when we visit the imprisoned, feed the poor, clothe the naked, give a drink to the thirsty, we do these things unto Him. He didn't say that we do these things in order to *please* Him, but that we do these things *to* Him. That means, in her view, that these people are Jesus in disguise."

Does Jim really believe that?

"Now that I have done it, I do," he said. "Why else would you do it? *How* else would you do it? There is no other reason."

Cheap Trip

For Charlie Schleicher, an attorney in Kansas City, the changes in his world were subtle at first. They started when his trip with us to St. Petersburg, Russia, took some unusual turns.

His motives for going may not have been ideal for a Heart to Heart trip, but that was OK with me. A lot of people volunteer to go on our airlifts, not because they want to serve others, but because they can be tourists in an unusual way. We make all of the arrangements for food and lodging, so some look at us as a type of low-budget travel agency. But since I know what happens to people when they are confronted with the needs of others, and what happens when they are given the opportunity to respond to those needs, I know that good things come out of what might be seen as selfish motives. In fact, before we ever left for Russia, Charlie told me, "I'm not going with a great humanitarian heart. I see this as a cheap way to get to Russia."

He heard about our trip through his Rotary Club. It was one of our first airlifts; we were going to Russia because their hospitals and clinics were experiencing severe shortages during the unusually bitter cold winter they were having. We needed volunteers to come with us and help distribute the medicine.

"I had promised my wife that we'd go on a trip that winter," Charlie said. "She was thinking Florida, so I didn't tell her at first that where we were going had an average temperature of 40 below."

The big attraction was that the trip was cheap. He could take his wife to Russia with us for a lot less than it cost to go to a resort. Then his plan was to ditch us and see the country as soon as he got there.

"My wife and I had no interest in visiting hospitals," he said.

His plan gathered steam. Soon there were several Rotary members who signed up to go with us who, we later found out, were planning to go their own way once they got there.

What Charlie and the others didn't anticipate was that they might actually enjoy our purpose for going.

On the trip over they got acquainted with some of our staff, and for the first few days in St. Petersburg, they attended our evening wrap-up sessions, where we talked about the day's events and tried to get a sense of what those events meant.

"They were really corny," he said. "It was incongruous that here were a bunch of businesspeople sitting around tables for what felt like story time at a Boy Scout campfire."

Still, he and the others remained.

"We got drawn into the vortex of the thing because there was a great spirit of purpose in the group," he said.

Charlie took in a lot of the Russian cultural events, but he eventually visited some hospitals. And even though he watched a ballet in the same palace where Catherine the Great watched ballet, his most vivid memory is of the hospital burn unit.

There was a badly burned child, about six years old, in a bed, and his wrists were tied to the bars on the sides so he wouldn't scratch his wounds. The boy was dying. The contrast of the ornate ballet auditorium and this ward was immense. Charlie couldn't believe how stark everything was in the hospital. There was nothing on the walls. And there were no parents.

Worse yet, the hospital had run out of burn cream. We knew of that shortage from a previous site inspection trip we had taken, so we had several pallets of the cream.

The Heart to Heart group with Charlie looked at the sad, little boy and felt his hopelessness. Then Charlie saw two from the group exchange glances. They reached into a bag and pulled out a small, fuzzy bear.

"I have never seen someone's countenance change as dramatically as that little boy's," Charlie said.

The doctor untied one of the boy's hands. The boy clutched the bear to his body, wiggling with joy.

"We had burn cream for his wounds, and a bear for his heart," Charlie said. "Who would have cared about him if we hadn't?" And while it was clear that the boy would not live long, his last few days would include a stuffed animal that meant someone cared about him.

Soon Charlie began reconsidering the meaning of some statements he had read for years.

"That experience in the hospital made me look at Jesus' command to follow Him," Charlie said. "When I look at that statement now, I see that it means to do what He does. And He reaches out in compassion and love to the needy."

Charlie's comfort zone, beliefs about how the world works, and plans for his vacation exploded. His trip to Russia suddenly became something else. It became a catalyst for finding meaning in his life—for looking to the needs of others, instead of just at his own.

Paul Clem, a volunteer on our Calcutta trip, said that he approaches his job in the U.S. differently as a result of working with the poor in India.

> *On the streets of Calcutta he watched people take fresh manure in their bare hands, flatten it into patties, and bake it over an open fire.*

On the streets of Calcutta he watched people take fresh manure in their bare hands, flatten it into patties, and bake it over an open fire. Then they tried to sell it for fuel.

"Since then I have had an uneasiness inside me," he said. "I feel as if I must do something. I can't just sit in my home and have food on demand. Things that are *wants* in my life are being sifted out. I used to think I *needed* to live in an expensive house. But why? Why?"

Working with these poorest of the poor has put a different spin on how he spends his life.

Now when he gets ready to make a presentation before a group of businesspeople, the usual nervousness kicks in, and he becomes tense. Then he thinks about Calcutta.

"This ain't nothin' compared to that," he said. "I'm not having to scratch just to stay alive. People around me have an outrageous sense of importance, and I tend to get caught up in that. But no matter how much pressure I feel, nothing compares to the streets of Calcutta."

Never Safe

At first this notion of having our world taken apart, of having our previous priorities and stereotypes replaced, can seem unsettling. It's similar to the way in which the children were nervous about meeting Aslan the lion in C. S. Lewis's book *The Lion, the Witch, and the Wardrobe,* one of the Chronicles of Narnia.

In the story, Mr. and Mrs. Beaver have just told the children that Aslan was King of the wood, the great lion, and son of the great Emperor-Beyond-the-Sea.

"Is he—quite safe?" asked Susan. "I shall feel rather nervous about meeting a lion."

Mrs. Beaver told the children that it was quite appropriate to be nervous.

"Then he isn't safe?" said Lucy.

"Safe?" said Mr. Beaver. "Don't you hear what Mrs. Beaver tells you? Who said anything about safe? 'Course he isn't safe. But he's good. He's the King, I tell you."

The children had never encountered something as big as Aslan. People who intentionally look for ways to respond to the needs of others face similar concerns about their own safety and comfort. And, as you read in chapter 8, meeting God and taking care of others are two very related acts. Eventually we get to the same position as Peter, the young boy in Lewis's story:

"I'm longing to see him," said Peter, "even if I do feel frightened" (pp. 75-76).

At this point some of you might be thinking that this approach to serving others—to having your world taken apart—could get pretty complicated. There is no clear-cut resolution to any of this. Where does it ultimately lead?

In his book *What Do You Say to a Hungry World?* Stanley Mooneyham says he frequently talks to God about matters like this—about his own fear of involvement, about the immensity of the needs, about the indifference of himself and others. The conversation sounds like this, Mooneyham wrote:

> *There is no clear-cut resolution to any of this. Where does it ultimately lead?*

"Lord, what do you want me to do about it? You want me to keep my head, I know. You haven't asked me—yet—to sell all I have and give to the poor. Sometimes I wish you would; it would make for an uncomplicated life. But would it really fulfill my commitment?"

And often the only answer Mooneyham says he gets are these words from God: "Follow Me."

Then Mooneyham says his best response is, "Renew a right spirit within me. Take the dimness of my soul away. . . . Bring me into the place of thy light."

"Go ahead," Mooneyham is saying, "take my world apart."

Not Normal, Not Predictable

But let's not presume that the only world being taken apart is ours—those who have committed their lives to being instruments of hope in a needy world. We have seen the worlds of the recipients taken apart as well as those of our volunteers. The worlds of the Vietnamese, the Russians, the children in orphanages in Calcutta. When the message of hope was delivered, the Vietnamese stereotype of an American was shattered. When Russian doctors saw that we had brought them burn cream for their suffering patients, the propaganda of Americans as evil evaporated. When children in orphanages no longer had to look at stuffed animals that were locked in a glass case, but could hold, sleep, and play with their own, their perceptions changed from "I am forgotten" to "Someone thought of me. I am loved."

While we were distributing medicine to some remote mountain villages in central China, we encountered a doctor who worked in his one-room clinic seven days a week. He had been the doctor for this region—responsible to thousands spread throughout the area—for more than 10 years. I talked with him about how he treated different injuries, and we stocked his supply room, which was virtually empty before we arrived.

When we finished visiting with him, he thanked us and said that, even after the supplies were gone, he would always remember that some strangers went out of their way to visit him and help his people. Then he told me he didn't know how much longer he would be serving this village. He said he had cancer of the colon.

I warned him that I was about to do something unusual. For the normally reserved Chinese people, a show of emotion is usually inappropriate. A simple bow to one another and a quick handshake is about as intimate as anyone gets. But I said, "One of the ways we show that we care about each other is that we hug them. So I am going to hug you."

And I did. This reserved, shy, dying doctor clung to me as if I were life itself. Then he hugged several others of our group. It wasn't a normal, predictable gesture on his part. But he responded that way because what he had received wasn't normal or predictable. He received medicine and something else—a message that said, "We care. There is hope." Life takes on a fresh perspective under those conditions.

> This reserved, shy, dying doctor clung to me as if I were life itself.

At the end of our time in China, the U.S. consul general, who reports directly to the U.S. ambassador to China, said to us, "You have done more for U.S./China relations than my staff and I have done in my entire time in China." Why? Because their understanding of Americans was limited to what they heard from Communist propaganda. And what our group of Americans understood about the Chinese was limited to our government statements about them. Then we saw each other face-to-face. That changed everything.

The story of the Good Samaritan is usually told from the perspective of the one responding to the person's need. But what do you think happened to the world of the victim? His physical world was violently taken apart by the robbers. My guess is that his inner world came apart, too, when he saw that someone provided for him when he was too weak to ask for help.

Sometimes circumstances occur in our lives, and we don't have any choice about whether our world will be taken apart. It happens whether we want it to or not. That's the way it was for Ray Mattix when he lost his company. Sometimes we have to look for ways to take our worlds apart. That's the way it was for Ray when he gazed into Ramondo's eyes.

Do we live in worlds where the boundaries are only as big as our towns, jobs, and churches?

Do we live in worlds where the boundaries are only as big as our towns, jobs, and churches? Worlds that are populated by those who earn, act, and look like us? Worlds that dismiss people of other cultures and races simply because they are different.

Is yours a finite world, bound by the notion that you are in the center? That's a very restrictive way to live. And not very accurate.

Ready for the dismantling?

10

HALF A TANGERINE

WHEN I WAS YOUNGER, I HAD A CERTAIN IMAGE OF what a miracle was. It usually had something to do with a Bible story where Moses or Elijah found themselves in a predicament, and God parted the Red Sea, made water gush from a rock, provided manna from heaven, had ravens bring food (the first humanitarian airlift recorded in history), or caused spontaneous combustion on a stone altar soaked with water.

Of course, those were Old Testament miracles. New Testament miracles included physical healings, raising people from the dead, and other events that resided in the arena of the spectacular, visible to everyone who was around.

As a physician, I have seen my share of miracles concerning people's physical conditions. What I mean by this is that I have witnessed occurrences where a disease or an injury that would act one way under normal circumstances acts a different way for some unexplained reason.

My view of what a miracle is has broadened considerably since I have been part of Heart to Heart. I have seen people act in different ways for some unexplained reason, just as I have seen illness change its expected course. And the great thing about miracles is that the more I look for them, the more I find them in everyday life.

This does not mean, though, that they are any less miraculous.

Nothing to Give

Consider what Michael Pitts encountered when he was at the Home for Dying Destitutes. A young man in his 20s lay on a cot trying to feed himself, but he was too weak. Lunch was a small bowl that had a mixture of rice, curry, and fish. Most of the man's food was smeared on the front of his shirt because his arms were too weak to get the spoon from the bowl to his mouth. Michael sat on the cot next to him and fed him. But within a few moments the dying man appeared agitated and held his mouth at a twisted angle.

A fish bone was caught in the back of the man's throat, and his arms were too frail to even pull the bone out. He could only whimper. Once Michael figured out the problem, he reached inside the man's mouth, found the offending bone, and removed it. The man didn't want any more rice and fish after that. But there was one more part of lunch. Each patient also had half of a tangerine. Michael pulled apart the sections and fed them to the man, who clearly enjoyed this part. A rare smile crossed his face.

While Michael fed him the last of the tangerine—really the only food that the man actually swallowed—he saw something waving.

Two cots from him was another emaciated man, weakly motioning to Michael. The second man had half a tangerine in his hand and gestured that Michael could take it and feed it to the man he was helping.

"I could scarcely keep myself together," Michael said. "The man two cots away clearly needed the nourishment, but he rose to the occasion in that moment in a most miraculous way."

I like the way Michael used the word "miraculous." It was one of those unexplained phenomena that I consider a miracle. And it was a gesture consistent with the sign I already mentioned in a back room at the Home for Dying Destitutes: Do Small Things with Great Love.

The man with half of a tangerine serves as a kind of role model for Michael now, for two reasons.

"I will never, never, ever say again that I have nothing to give," he said. "If a dying man can offer a few sections of fruit to relieve the suffering of another dying man, then I will always have something to give."

The other lesson Michael learned is that the miraculous can also be commonplace.

"There are plenty of opportunities here, in the moment, to rise to the occasion of the moment, as that man did," he said.

It is a conclusion similar to the one John Wesley came to when he wrote, "He who governed the world before I was born shall take care of it likewise when I am dead. My part is to improve the present moment."

Many miraculous events have taken place to allow us to conduct these airlifts that relieve suffering of those receiving medicine and provide meaning to those who distribute it. Having 40 or more clearances from government agencies in India was a miracle. Getting the Vietnam government to give us permission to come to their country was a miracle. Giving protection to our convoy of medicine to war-torn Sarajevo was a miracle.

A lot of public posturing had been going on in both the U.S. and China about China's human rights record.

Here's one that affected our most recent airlift—to the Szechwan Province of China.

The Looks of Things

Barbi Moore and a few others from Heart to Heart met for a long time with members of the economic division of the U.S. Embassy in Beijing, trying to get the necessary clearances for our project there. The embassy staff was not very encouraging. The political climate there was not conducive to this sort of thing, they told our group.

A lot of public posturing had been going on in both the U.S. and China about China's human rights record, about its takeover of Hong Kong, about its persecution of religious groups, about its international trade practices. The U.S. government was afraid of doing something that would be misconstrued as helping a Communist country. So without saying no to the idea of the China airlift, they made it clear that it was a long shot at best. As Barbi put it, "It was not a good meeting. We felt that the doors were closing in our face."

Leaving that division's office, they tried to remember what door they had come in. The division is in one building of several that make up the embassy compound, and each building has several doors and hallways. They chose a direction and proceeded toward the exit with their heads down, very discouraged.

But as they started out the door, they ran into someone on his way in. "Jack!" Barbi nearly screamed his name. "Barbi!" he yelled back. The two hugged and greeted each other like two long-lost friends. It was Jack Gosnell, the former U.S. consul general in St. Petersburg, Russia, with whom we had worked on two previous airlifts.

"What are you doing here?" Barbi asked.

"From the looks of things," he said, gesturing to her group, "I'm organizing another airlift for Heart to Heart!"

The U.S. government had transferred Jack to be the minister counselor for economic affairs in China just a few months before. He had no idea that we were planning an airlift to his new country or that we had just been talking to the people who work for him. But when he saw our delegates in the lobby, he quickly figured it out.

One of the people who had just moments before been discouraging the effort said to Barbi, "I think we're going to start this meeting over."

"Follow me," Jack said.

They went back to the very office where our group had heard something akin to "No way." Jack told the embassy workers that we were legitimate and that they would offer whatever support and encouragement they could to make the airlift happen.

"The very people who offered us no hope were now going to make it happen," said Barbi. "I'm comfortable using the word *miracle*."

Another event we like to call a miracle was something that *didn't* happen. The news media in Calcutta did not appreciate what we were doing there. They were sure that we had ulterior motives in bringing in medicine and supplies. When the news-

papers found out that we were coming and that the government had waived the usual customs fees on our shipments,
headlines screamed that the government gave away millions in
revenues for a bunch of outdated junk. It wasn't outdated, of
course, but it's hard to change a person's mind with facts after
his mind is made up.

It also infuriated them to think that their government was
accepting charity. They were offended that we thought they
needed medical assistance. One look around the city could
make anyone certain of the need, but some of the influential
people of Calcutta still publicly deny that there is a health problem there. So the largest medical airlift in India's history was
not a welcome sight to them.

The media hostility got so bad that we finally conducted a
news conference to explain our purpose for coming. They
didn't believe us when we originally said that we were coming
simply out of love. When people don't believe your story, they
feel free to make up their own. We dreaded this confrontation.
We didn't see how it could help, and we knew it could backfire.
But on the day of the news conference, the taxi drivers went on
strike, and hundreds of reporters from outside Calcutta were
unable to attend. Those from Calcutta showed up with their ac-
cusations, but it could have been much worse. I like to think of
it as Pharaoh's army being stranded on the other side of the Red
Sea. Drowning them wasn't necessary when delaying them was
just as effective!

These kinds of changes in the usual order of things don't
have to be on a grand scale for them to still be miraculous. And
sacred.

Holy Week

Jim Wise, an audiologist from Kansas City, was with us on
the Calcutta airlift. His company brought materials for con-
structing a sound booth along with testing materials and molds
so that he and some others could make hearing aids. They fitted
more than 200 people with hearing aids in just a few days. One
old Hindu man, though, stands out in Jim's experience.

He had been waiting in their makeshift clinic all day. It

took that long to get people tested and fitted, and then they had to come back another day to pick up their hearing aids. The day this man returned was Holy Thursday, the day of Jesus' last supper before He was betrayed and crucified.

When the man finally received his hearing aid, he was delighted that he could hear again. "May God bless you during your holiday season," the man said to Jim.

"Here was a Hindu man who gave me a Christian blessing during one of the most important times of the Christian faith," Jim explains. "It was his way of saying that religion and race weren't the issue—gratitude was. Human contact and love rose above it all."

The encounter reminds me of one Jesus had that is recorded in Luke 17:11-19. He was on His way to Jerusalem, and as He entered a village, He came upon 10 men with leprosy. Stories like this take on new meaning for me now that I have been with lepers in Calcutta and Vietnam. No one will have anything to do with them. They are not welcomed outside the wall of their own compounds. If they *are* seen outside their village, people even today will throw things at them, chase them back to their villages, or keep their distance and shout insults. The way lepers were treated in Jesus' day has not changed much.

Even Jesus seemed surprised at what the man did, and at what the others did not do.

The lepers who saw Jesus stood a ways off and shouted, "Master, take pity on us." He did and told them to show themselves to the priest. As they went on their way, they were healed. One of the 10 turned back and sought out Jesus to thank Him. Then the Bible drops in a statement that strikes me as very powerful: "And he was a Samaritan." Once again, it is the lowest of the low—the lepers—and an enemy of the Jews, on top of it, who shows gratitude.

Even Jesus seemed surprised at what the man did, and at

what the others did not do. He asks, "Could none be found to come back and give praise to God except this foreigner?"

It was the Samaritan thanking the Jew—rising above the politics and race—because he realized that gratitude was the only appropriate response. The other 9 missed out on something wonderful. True, their leprosy was cured, and they could move back among the regular citizens. But they didn't have an encounter that took them beyond disease the way the one man did. In these additional encounters of love and gratitude, where true miracles occur and are often overlooked, the commonplace becomes holy.

In our case it was the Hindu thanking the Christian with a Christian blessing, during a Christian Holy Week. And it happened on a day that Jesus turned things upside down—disrupted the natural order of things—by taking a towel and basin and washing the disciples' feet. That one act destroyed the social order. The King of the Jews, the Son of God, Rabbi, Master, Teacher, exercised His position in the world by serving others.

"When we share in God's compassion, a whole new way of living opens itself to us," writes Henri Nouwen (*Compassion*, 21).

As we have discovered through Heart to Heart activities, entering into the sufferings of others produces holy moments. Mother Teresa made this discovery long before we did. Jesus lived it.

Sacred Encounters, Magnificent Obsessions

My daughter Erin experienced it in Calcutta too. She was 17 at the time and used to seeing needy people. At home I made it part of my routine, while my kids were growing up, to take them with me when I did hospital rounds on weekends and holidays when they were out of school. But it was in the Home for Dying Destitutes that Erin experienced a sacred moment.

If I could add to the sign, I would write: and the House of *Clarity*. It shows us what life is at its root—joy and suffering living together, not in competition, but in acceptance.

When our group was ready to leave the home at the end of

the day, we looked for Erin, but she wasn't with us. So we went back in to find her. We watched as she held an old, frail, blind woman and tried to feed her. But the woman didn't want to be fed. She only wanted to be held. We watched as Erin finally put the food down, cradled her, and gently stroked her hair. The woman went completely limp in Erin's arms.

"In the middle of the drool, the gunk, and the smelly, dying people, I couldn't think of a more appropriate place to be on Easter weekend," Susie Shellenberger, editor of *Brio* magazine, who was with us, said. "Watching Erin in the middle of this, I said to myself, 'Susie, remember how this smells. Remember these details. Freeze this moment. Don't let it be an image that you have to conjure up.'

"Then, at the end of the room I saw the basin of water they use to bathe these people," Susie added. "Above the basin is a sign that says, This Is the Body of Christ."

Erin rose to the moment in an everyday, miraculous way. Something beyond herself was at work.

In the 1950s a movie classic was filmed titled *The Magnificent Obsession.* In the movie there is a wonderful scene in which an older, wiser character named Edward Randolph is trying to explain to the younger playboy character, Bob Merrick, that there is more to life than looking out for one's own self-interests. Merrick asks what's wrong with looking out for himself, and Randolph replies that it is important to "do what you were meant to do."

And what is that? Merrick asks. "Be of service to people," Randolph said. "Find people who need you, and help them."

But Randolph isn't unrealistic about what he tells Merrick.

> "In the middle of the drool, the gunk, and the smelly, dying people, I couldn't think of a more appropriate place to be on Easter weekend."

He also warns, "Be surprised at what follows when you try this way of life. This is dangerous stuff. One of the fellows who used it went to the Cross."

The magnificent obsession articulated by Randolph is a description of how we can live our lives—not out of duty or obligation, but out of love and a desire to "do what you were meant to do." As a result, something miraculous happens.

Dr. Nishan Kazazian, the Los Angeles dentist I mentioned in a previous chapter, understands this. His colleague, Dr. Gary Kevorkian, started a mobile dental clinic, taking Kazazian and other dentists to Armenia after the devastating earthquake there in 1988 and after the Soviet Union began its collapse. They take a mobile dental clinic so they can do extractions, cleanings, fillings, and other dental work we would consider routine in this country. They go twice a year and have gone with Heart to Heart in recent years.

In Armenia they see more patients in one day than they see in two weeks in the U.S.

"We use the assembly-line method," he said. "One administers the anesthetic, another does the preparation, another does the extraction, another does the filling, and another does the mop-up work." With this method it is possible to extract rotted or dead teeth from 60 people in one day.

Doctors and dentists have in recent years done their work— even surgery— without being able to give their patients any painkiller.

After several days of work under these conditions, you would think the dentists would return to their practice in the U.S. exhausted, needing a vacation.

"It is the most energizing thing I do all year," Nishan said. "I come back stronger and more motivated than ever."

The reason is that the interaction between the dentists and their patients makes them feel alive.

When they first started doing this, the patients would come filled with terror or alcohol—sometimes both. The country has been under a blockade from all of its bordering neighbors for years, causing unbelievable shortages of fuel, food, medicine, and medical supplies. So doctors and dentists have in recent years done their work—even surgery—without being able to give their patients any painkiller. He remembers one young boy who came back to the clinic to give Nishan a candy bar. "All I did was fill some holes in his teeth," Nishan said. "He came back with something that took a great sacrifice. Given what that chocolate bar cost him, he gave me far more than I gave him."

These holy moments aren't always this clear at first, though. Ed Holly is a San Diego dentist who went with Heart to Heart to Armenia, and the trip was a different kind of work at first from what he planned.

"I admit I was bitter at the beginning," he said. "I went there because I wanted to practice dentistry and help people," he said. "But it seemed that everything kept getting in the way of doing just that."

While trying to get into Armenia with all of our supplies, our plane landed in the Ukraine to refuel. But the government in Kyiv wouldn't allow us to take off again. Once they saw what we were carrying, they tried to confiscate it so they could either use it in their own country, which also has shortages, or sell it on the black market. We have heard about groups that bring medicine to countries where they do not personally oversee its distribution, and the drugs are sometimes sold on the black market before the groups even get back home. We are careful that we personally see where all of the supplies go. So we debated with the people in Kyiv for several hours, and finally the U.S. State Department representatives traveling with us intervened on our behalf.

This delay in Kyiv caused a problem for us in Armenia, though. We had told the people there that we would arrive at 8 A.M., and that we would need their help unloading the supplies. But we lost a lot of time in Kyiv, so we didn't arrive in Armenia until 3 P.M. Our helpers didn't know where we were, and had already gone home. That meant we had to do it ourselves. We worked until 4 A.M. the next day, taking pallets off the plane, then taking boxes off the pallets and putting them in trucks. In a freezing rain.

We got a few hours sleep, then drove most of the next day to different clinics and unloaded the trucks.

"Nobody was there to help us," Ed Holly said. "It is 6,000-foot elevation, raining, and we're the moving crew again. I had been traveling three days and hadn't done a bit of dentistry."

But then one of the interpreters inquired, Why were the doctors doing the work of peasants?

"The first thing out of my mouth was that God wasn't concerned about someone's position or number of college degrees," Ed said. "I told her that loving God meant doing for others what needed to be done, whatever it was. That got us into a wonderful conversation about what it means to be a human being and what it means to love God.

"Then it dawned on me: I'm feeling sorry for myself because I'm not pulling teeth, yet I'm standing here reaching across all sorts of barriers, describing what love is. It wasn't very hard to figure out the meaning of that encounter."

Later on that same trip, another member of our group had her own sacred encounter. Zandra Fennell was the director of professional services for McNeil Consumer Products Laboratories in Pennsylvania at the time. Her role on this airlift was to document for McNeil that the medicine the company donated actually reached its intended destination. But it quickly became more than that for her.

> The people of Armenia truly have nothing, and it seems that no one knows it. It's as if the earthquake of 1988 just happened yesterday.

She said going to Armenia was like going into outer space and discovering that people were living and barely surviving there, but no one else knew about it. The people of Armenia truly have nothing, and it seems that no one knows it. It's as if the earthquake of 1988 just happened yesterday. People there live in tin, makeshift shacks. There is no electricity or running water in the towns where we were.

"In the U.S., no matter how low you are in society, you can get someplace," Zandra said. "If there is a flood, you can get some shelter. In Armenia there is no place to go."

Zandra remembers going to a small store near where she stayed and buying three one-liter bottles of Coke for several of us to drink that night. They cost $10 total. "I spent what an Armenian makes in a month for Coke for one night," she said. Bread is rationed there. Each family gets two small loaves per day. The bread is handed out at 6 A.M. each day. The line begins forming at 5 A.M.

This kind of hardship made an impact on Zandra and, in a church service in nearby Kazakhstan, her perspective on people living in this region and on her own life became clearer.

It was a service in Russian and English, held in a school building.

"The people sang heartily—they were so excited about being able to worship openly after doing so in secret for years under the Soviet system," she said.

While she was in the service, something dawned on her. For the past eight years in her home church in Pennsylvania, the pastor would light a candle every Sunday, name a church that was suffering in the Soviet Union, and lead the congregation in a prayer specifically for that church. Then he asked the congregation to remember that specific church in their prayers during the week. Zandra's home church is a Presbyterian church. She was worshiping this particular day in a Presbyterian church that had suffered persecution from the Soviets during the period when her home church was praying.

Zandra turned to the woman translating for her and said, "We prayed for this church back home." The woman smiled broadly and replied, "We always knew."

"She told me they knew that people around the world were praying for them, and it was this knowledge that helped give them the courage to keep worshiping, even when it was against the law," Zandra said. "She said that we gave them hope."

She had watched someone light a candle for these people, she had prayed for them, she shared in their suffering, and now she was worshiping with them. All unplanned. All sacred.

"It was an experience I will never forget," she said.

The kinds of miracles I have described have a pretty sizable fault, though. They aren't very efficient. They take a lot of time and effort, and they affect only the individuals involved in that sacred moment. But they are filled with a quality of love so great that it makes me want to recognize those moments more frequently and live in that love.

> The kinds of miracles I have described have a pretty sizable fault, though. They aren't very efficient.

As Michael Pitts concluded about the man offering his food, it wasn't spectacular like the sun standing still or bread coming down from heaven. But it *was* miraculous.

"I always thought a miracle was a big thing like what Heart to Heart was doing in Calcutta—a $12 million airlift—or a permanent thing like those audiologists helping people hear for the rest of their lives," he said. "But I personally never saw the impact of either one of those."

When he looked up from the cot where he was sitting and saw a man give the only thing left to give, though, Michael saw miracles in a new light.

"I'll never be able to do $12 million worth of anything," he said. "But I'll always be good for at least a half of a tangerine."

He discovered the meaning of love in everyday life. And that's miraculous.

11

WEENIE ROAST

THE LATE KAREKINE THE FIRST HAD A SECRET, BUT HE
didn't know that we knew. He was the highest-ranking official
in the Armenian Orthodox Church, one of the first churches
established after Christianity began. His official title was the
catholicos, but a lot of people simply called him the pope of the
Armenian church.

And we knew something about him that many in Armenia
didn't know: he liked American hot dogs.

When we conducted our airlift to Armenia in 1995, it was
partly because it looked as if the massive earthquake of 1988
had just occurred. The availability of electricity and running
water was sporadic throughout the country several years later.
The destruction of buildings and roadways was still largely un-
repaired. The government, newly formed after the collapse of
the Soviet Union, was experiencing severe shortages, so a national rebuilding project was nothing more than a desire. And
even if they *were* able to organize and rebuild, they share bor-
ders with countries that consider them the enemy, so supplies
are difficult and expensive to obtain.

It was a country that could justify being completely hopeless.

More than a Celebration

As I mentioned in the last chapter, Heart to Heart connected with a group of dentists from Los Angeles that had been going to Armenia with a mobile dental clinic for the last few years.
It was on one of those previous trips that they learned the
catholicos's secret about hot dogs. The story goes that, while he

147

was doing graduate study in the United States, he was in New York, hurrying from one meeting to another. He hadn't had time for lunch that day and was very hungry, so at an intersection he looked out the window of his limousine and saw a street vendor selling hot dogs. He sent the driver out for one, and it was love at first bite.

Knowing that, we decided that our trip to Armenia would be more than just an airlift of medical supplies to help the needy. We would include hot dogs for the church's top brass and make a party out of it.

Toward the end of our stay in Armenia, after supplying hospitals and clinics with much-needed medicine and supplies, and after doing dental work on hundreds of needy Armenian poor, we visited the seat of the Armenian Orthodox Church, with the oldest functioning seminary in the world, at the foot of Mount Ararat. People from the seminary took us on a tour and showed us ancient art—beautiful paintings, tapestries, icons, relics, jewelry, and sculptures—along with a splinter of wood in an ornate case. They believe the wood came from the cross on which Jesus was crucified. It felt as if we had traveled to the end of the world and almost the beginning of civilization.

We then rolled out the picnic items. Hot dogs, along with mustard, ketchup, buns, potato chips, salad, and soda.

Then seminarians, ranging in ages from 16 to 20, dressed in dark, tattered frocks, sang us songs. Ancient hymns, in an ancient language, in an ancient land that is believed to be the region where Noah's ark landed after the worldwide Flood thousands of years before. Then the catholicos came out of his chambers, with his white hair and flowing white beard. He was surrounded by other high-ranking church officials. They were dressed in the robes and hats that designate their place in the church hierarchy. We called him

Your Excellency, and he greeted us and thanked us for coming. He told about the difficulty of being a Christian nation surrounded by Muslim countries like Turkey, Azerbaijan, and Iran, and asked us to pray for peace. We prayed together in what felt like an incredible connection of the ancient to the present.

The dentists then rolled out the picnic items. Hot dogs (packed in dry ice), along with mustard, ketchup, buns, potato chips, salad, and soda. We spread it all out on red-checkered tablecloths. When Karekine the First saw what we had done, he was thrilled! He considered it something special that someone remembered about his U.S. experience. He made sure that all of the seminarians had hot dogs, too, and many of them returned for several helpings. "How many people can say that they've had a weenie roast with the pope?" someone remarked.

The picnic made an impact on all of us. It was fun to conduct what is probably a 100-year-old American tradition on a site where civilization has been for thousands of years. And it was fun because it was a celebration of what had been occurring between our group and the people our group came to serve.

More than just a celebration about hot dogs and medicine, it was a celebration of involvement and contact. It is one of the great lessons we have learned at Heart to Heart: Doing things for others leads to joy!

Surprised by Joy

We've learned that joy often surprises us at the most unexpected moments in the some of the most unusual places. When we were in Calcutta unloading a truck filled with boxes of supplies at one of Mother Teresa's Missions of Charity, it was one of those times.

The driveway from the street to the entrance of the orphanage was too narrow for us to drive the truck right up to the door, but we got it as close as we could. As I said before, we formed a bucket brigade to pass the boxes along. Some of the group were in the truck, handing boxes down to others on the street, and the boxes went through about 20 pairs of hands before they were handed up to those stationed on the stairs lead-

ing to the entrance. The chain of people stretched from the city
street, through the courtyard, up the stairs, and to a storage
room in the orphanage.

The noise of Calcutta streets is so constant that we had to
shout to hear each other. Loud truck and car engines, vehicle
horns, people shouting—all are complicated by not enough
room for a fraction of what tries to inch along the streets. The
streets of Calcutta were not built with the idea that millions of
people would use them for everything ranging from transportation to toilets; yet there they are, all day long, at a deafening level.

Combine the assault on the ears with the grime and grit of
thick, dirty, pungent air, in a climate where you sweat constantly and profusely, in a culture that doesn't have enough clean
water or soap to bathe regularly, and you have a picture of what
our assembly line at the orphan-
age was like.

As we finished unloading the
truck, we desperately needed relief. Just before the heat and noise
and grime caved in on us, we
heard something rise above it all.
It was the sisters from the mission—they were singing. They
sang about God's love that gives
us love for one another. And they
sang about how they loved us.

Some of us

couldn't stop crying.

We watched

as these sisters,

dressed in their

blue and white saris,

sang with enthusiasm,

gratitude, and joy.

Some of us couldn't stop crying. We watched as these sisters,
dressed in their blue and white
saris, sang with enthusiasm, gratitude, and joy. What made it even
more poignant was that everyone
knew we would be there for just a
few days, but that they would be
there for the rest of their lives.

It was a spontaneous, sacred moment of celebration.

One volunteer said he was crying tears of confusion, longing, and joy. He remembers thinking, "There is something to learn here about what is important. They're the happy ones and yet they are the ones staying. I was the one feeling sad, and I knew that I'd be in an American restaurant in a week, talking about it." Over the years, we've heard the same thing from people who have invested their lives in others for the duration. Yes, they face hardship; yes, they miss their families; yes, they miss the conveniences of modern American life; yes, they get hot and hungry; yes, they get overwhelmed by the size of the need; and yes, they are happy to stay in this place of suffering indefinitely because they see the world through God's eyes.

Serving God by serving one another is our responsibility, I have said previously in this book. Mother Teresa called it a privilege. This kind of service leads to joy and can even break into celebration! What we experienced at the orphanage was the purest joy we had ever known.

This may be a different way of looking at celebration than how you have looked at it before. It isn't the kind of celebration where we remove ourselves from hardship or reminders of our normal living conditions and replace them with parties, singing, dancing, leisure, and other activities of escape. This isn't the celebration that happens when we avoid life for a while. I'm talking about the celebration that occurs when we *immerse* ourselves in life.

> It isn't the kind of celebration where we remove ourselves from hardship or reminders of our normal living conditions and replace them with parties, singing, dancing, leisure, and other activities of escape.

"Celebration can really come about only where fear and love, joy and sorrow, tears and smiles can exist together," writes

Henri Nouwen. Celebration is the result of seeing paradoxical things together, he says (*Seeds of Hope,* 35). When we celebrate a wedding, it is for the union and the departure. We celebrate death for the gained liberty and the lost friendship. A birth makes one free to breathe on his or her own, but the baby has lost the safety of the mother's body. In other words, conflicting emotions are intertwined with each moment. That's what makes them something to celebrate—they come from the realization that life and death, pain and sorrow, fear and love, tears and smiles, exist together.

Moments like These

We saw this occur in one of the activities we had planned during our stay in Calcutta. The people of the Calcutta Rotary wanted to show their appreciation for our visit, so they arranged for us to see a nationally revered Indian dance and music group. It is led by Ananda Shankar, the nephew of Indian musician Ravi Shankar, whose sitar music was very popular in the U.S. in the 1960s.

We saw the performance in one of the great halls in Calcutta and were impressed by the artists' abilities, although we felt a little self-conscious about being part of this private audience. To our delight, we learned that the performers planned to take the production to a leprosy village we had visited earlier in the week. We knew that the residents there *never* have seen anything as wonderful as what we just witnessed that evening.

Within a few days, a sun-baked, open area in the village was transformed into its own concert hall.

The Missionaries of Charity had developed this particular village as a haven for the outcast. The 700 residents grow their own crops, weave all of the clothes for the sisters, and build their own prostheses. They are a self-sufficient colony, with all residents engaged in meaningful work.

And yet, they are banned by their culture from interacting with people outside the village because of their disease. They are incarcerated. So you can see why we were surprised when this group of national heroes—the equivalent of rock stars in the U.S.—said they would perform for these people whom their society rejects.

Within a few days, a sun-baked, open area in the village was transformed into its own concert hall. Residents made enormous tentlike coverings and suspended them on poles over hundreds of chairs. They constructed a stage, and they dressed as if they were attending an elaborate wedding. And when the troupe arrived, they couldn't stop cheering and applauding. The residents of this leprosy village had never seen anything like this.

Neither had the performers. At first they were reluctant to interact much with the residents. They seemed taken back by the magnitude of the suffering, and acted afraid. They did what we did when we first visited there—they kept to themselves.

But soon the warmth of the residents overcame the fear of the performers, and the result was a performance that the world would have paid top dollar to see. It was spirited, inspired, intense, and wildly appreciated.

Who had the most fun of anyone that day? The performers. They had broken outside of the cultural walls and stereotypes, moved past their expectations and fears, risked something, and given of themselves for someone else. The result was a true celebration of service and contact! It was full of what Nouwen described as fear and love existing together. It was also rich and poor existing together, if only for a few hot, sticky, wonderful hours.

We celebrate in moments like this because these are the times in our lives when we live out our true purpose. We recognize that this is what life is *supposed* to be. Since we were created to desire significance, when it happens, we celebrate! One of the most exciting declarations someone can make is, "I made a difference."

In the movie *City of Joy,* the doctor character played by Patrick Swayze considers whether he should stay in Calcutta in a clinic that has to beg or connive for every possible supply and coin, or to return to his successful medical practice in Houston, where he would once again be one of the world's elite. He is considering this question, not coincidentally, during a wedding celebration. Earlier, the doctor had sewn up the bride's face when gangsters sliced her with a razor blade to teach those at the clinic a lesson. Now she was marrying a good man, and the village was rejoicing in the new union.

"I have never felt more alive than I do right now," the doctor declared, as he decided to remain in Calcutta.

In the many airlifts we have done at Heart to Heart, I have heard dozens of people make that same statement. One man, who had been a Vietnam War protester in the 1960s, said at the end of a day of working in a leprosy village in Vietnam, "Except for my birth and my wedding, this is the most important day of my life."

Why? He discovered that he was truly alive. And that discovery came when he entered into the lives of people who needed help. He was created to actively serve other human beings. And when he got to do it, he was alive and full of joy.

We saw this in a poignant way when we conducted our airlift to China. Remember that at the time this was a country that seemed to be on the brink of a cold war with the U.S. over political, economic, and social issues. They were allies during World War II only because they had a common enemy. And occasionally something happened where it looked as if the countries were trying to be friendly, such as China allowing giant pandas to live and attempt to breed in U.S. zoos. But in all practicality, the two countries treated each other with a great deal of suspicion.

But when we came in with 40 tons of medicine and supplies, they celebrated, and so did we! On the tarmac of the Chengdu airport was a military band and a group of children that gave each of us a picture they had drawn and a bouquet of flowers. We had gifts for them too. The sight of our volunteers kneeling, receiving a gift, and then giving a gift to these overjoyed children, is locked in my memory forever. There was something to celebrate for each of us. The breaking down of cultural, political, and language barriers—however temporary—

was worth acknowledging and enjoying. And why were they broken down? Because people decided it was worth the risk to get involved with the needs of someone else. We celebrated that we had more in common than we had uncommon. And, however briefly, we felt significant.

For that moment, we all understood why this contact with strangers was a good thing.

Why? Because we were living our true purpose, which is to love God and love one another. To love God *by* loving one another.

Barbi Moore and her husband, Harlan, drove the point home unmistakably that night. The Chinese government sponsored a banquet for us at a Chengdu hotel as another way of thanking us for paying our own way to bring these crucial medicines and supplies to their people. There was some traditional Chinese entertainment after dinner, and word got around that Barbi and Harlan were good singers. The evening had been full of Chinese food and Chinese entertainment. But they asked if the Moores would do a song at the end.

Barbi and Harlan communicate powerfully when they sing. And the song they chose was ideal for that event, that evening.

The chorus is:
Love in any language, straight from the heart,
Pulls us all together, never apart.
And once we learn to speak it, all the world will hear,
Love in any language fluently spoken here.
Two beautiful lines from one of the verses say:
Maybe when we realize how much there is to share,
*We'll find too much in common to pretend it isn't there.**

As I looked across the banquet room of U.S. and Chinese government and business leaders, they acted as if they were

---

*"Love in Any Language." Words and music by Jon Mohr and John Mays. Copyright © 1986 Jonathan Mark Music/Sutton Hill Music/Birdwing Music.

parched, and Barbi and Harlan were giving them a cool drink. The ovation at the end of the song was loud and long. For that moment, we all understood why this contact with strangers was a good thing—because it was consistent with the way we are made. We are created to love God and others, to serve God by serving others. Connecting to that purpose, however briefly, creates joy!

The U.S. ambassador to China at the time, James Sasser, was there. So was the secretary general of China's Szechwan Province—the highest-ranking official over the 110 million people. All of them wiped tears from their eyes at the end of the song. After the banquet Ambassador Sasser said to me, "You have no idea how much good you have done for the relationship between our two countries."

In Every Language

In the smaller towns and villages we visited, similar exhibitions of celebration occurred. Some had taken some planning, but some were spontaneous, such as when the deputy minister of health of one of the cities wrote and sang a song for us on the spur of the moment. The people of the town were delighted to see him do this, as were we. Love in any language was fluently spoken there.

People celebrate when they bridge the countless things that separate us, such as health, politics, lifestyle, culture, race, and religion. It's a remarkable thing when these differences give way to a common purpose—to make a difference in each other's lives.

What is the root of this desire to make a difference? Pascal said there is a God-shaped vacuum in each of us. This is more than just the desire to do an occasional good deed. It is more than emotion. A tear shed for a lonely widow is emotion, Brennan Manning says. When that tear is combined with writing her a letter, knocking on her door, or calling her on the telephone, it is love.

We can show love to those who love us and still not find significance. Experiencing significance, then joy, happens when we go beyond traditional barriers to love. E. Stanley Jones tells of a visitor at a medical station in India watching a nurse attend the sores of a person with leprosy. The visitor watched in horror and said that she wouldn't do that for a million dollars. The nurse replied that she wouldn't either, but she would do it for God for free.

That nurse had discovered the secret of viewing others as God views them, in whatever condition they may be at the moment. This is love that demands celebration!

There is a frustration in loving like this. It never seems to be enough. We may provide medicine to someone in need and celebrate that we are both created in the image of God. Then we leave, knowing we haven't changed their condition very much. They'll be hungry again. They still have leprosy. They don't have running water. Difficult conditions remain the same.

There is a frustration in loving like this. It never seems to be enough.

We've seen that our goal cannot be to solve something. It must be to *be* something. So we look to one another and, in meeting others' needs, find our purpose.

Throughout this book I have told stories of what we have learned about living lives that are intentionally ordered to get involved in the needs of others. It is a mandate I believe comes from Jesus' own words in Matt. 25, as well as the rest of the Bible. And I see it confirmed every day when I witness someone getting outside of their traditional boundaries to do something for someone else. Sometimes this involvement comes with a sizable sacrifice of time and money, but usually it doesn't. There will always be enough resources to do God's work. You will always have enough to do something for others.

Somewhere along the line most of us have believed the verse that said, "God helps those who help themselves." The problem is that isn't a verse in the Bible. Ben Franklin said it, not Jesus.

We all have excess, whether it looks like it or not at any given moment. We have seen firsthand that most of the world barely scratches by. Some made their last scratches today because there isn't enough where they are. They simply can't help themselves.

Ordering our lives to take others' needs into account is a responsibility, a duty, and a privilege all at the same time. We haven't relieved all the suffering in the world, and we won't try. But we do what we can, and when we do, it is a great source of joy.

As a rabbi friend said in Washington, D.C., "The most powerful lessons are those that travel from heart to heart."

To those who have never considered this concept, it is nonsense. "Hope unbelieved is always considered nonsense," Jim Wallis wrote. And yet it is hope that is the door between one reality and another.

Working to meet the needs of others looks foolish at first, because it is measured according to how much we *accomplish.* But we can't measure significance and purpose using external instruments. Life isn't about solving problems any more than Heart to Heart is about providing pills. It's about people connecting with one another. It's about love—in any language.

12

CROSSING THE LINE

WORD HAD APPARENTLY GOTTEN OUT TO THE VILlage. We were in central China and had spent the day distributing boxes of medicine and supplies to hospitals, starting with a large municipal hospital, and with each facility getting farther and farther into the country. Each place we went had huge crowds made up of mostly curious people from the town we were visiting. And after we finished greeting the medical staff and unloading the trucks, we mingled with the crowd that had gathered, greeting them, giving them small gifts, communicating as best we could.

I don't know what the problem was; maybe it was taking too much time, or maybe our government escorts didn't want us interacting with anyone other than the medical personnel. Or maybe this last village we were visiting that day had a reputation for being rowdy. But something was clearly different by the time we got there.

This time, when we pulled up in front of the village clinic, the crowd had turned out as they had in other locations. But they stood off at a distance, not daring to cross in front of the government officials that had arrived before us. There were hundreds of people—kids, parents, the elderly—all crowded and noisy and curious, but behind an invisible line.

The government escorts didn't look mean. They didn't have guns or any other visible weapons. They wore suits similar to the one I was wearing, and looked like businessmen. But it was clear that they had authority, and no one considered challenging it. Just a handful of men kept these hundreds of curious people away from us without lifting a hand or raising a voice.

What these men hadn't anticipated, though, was that my dad was part of our delegation on this China airlift.

Now in his 70s, he still has more energy than many groups of people combined. He *ran* up the steps when we visited the Great Wall of China. He bought *every single* handkerchief that had a panda on it from a large department store so he could give them as gifts when he got back to the U.S. A crowd of salespeople surrounded him, delighted to offer him more things to buy. There's nothing he'd rather do than give someone a gift.

So he wasn't about to let a couple of guys in suits keep these rural Chinese onlookers from receiving what he had brought them. None of his gifts were life-sustaining medicine, like the boxes we were carrying into the clinic. These were pieces of candy, stickers, pencils, pads of paper, small toys—stuff that would be gone or broken in minutes. But they were destined for these people, many of whom had never seen an American.

He didn't wave these people to himself, though. My dad was sensitive enough to see that they had been told to stay back. He went to them instead. No one said *we* couldn't cross the invisible line to *them*.

When he did, the people were delighted. He had something for every child. I've seen him do this a thousand times with American kids. This time seemed no different. He, and they, acted as if there were no language barrier. Because he had gone to them, he erased that invisible line drawn before we had arrived. They laughed, shook hands, and shared the delight of being together. Even the government escorts seemed pleased. They proudly wore the pins my dad put on their lapels.

Norm Shoemaker, also one of the volunteers with us in China, didn't hesitate to follow my dad's lead. He had a bag of candy also and went toward another part of the crowd. The children were excited, of course, and gathered around him the way they did my dad. Just as he reached into his bag and handed out the very last piece of candy to an anxious child, he looked up and saw that across the road stood a young girl partially hidden by the shade of a doorway. He could tell she was different. He suspected she was a Down syndrome child. She had been watching everything from a distance—the excited kids, the gifts, the enthusiasm of seeing all of these strangers from another country.

Norm walked toward her, his mind racing. "What can I give her? I just gave away my last piece of candy!" he thought. Then he remembered that he still had a Heart to Heart sticker in his pocket. The girl didn't retreat as he approached, but remained still, leaning against the doorway, now even more clearly afflicted. Norm pulled the sticker out of his pocket and motioned to her that he wanted to put it on her. As he pulled the paper off the back, the girl straightened up, ready to receive it.

When he finished placing the sticker on her shirt, she stood at attention. Norm said that it was as if she were saying, "I don't know what organization I just joined, but I am very proud to be a member." Then she whirled around and ran excitedly into the building.

Remembering We Came

This is a village where the work of the adults is backbreaking. Its primary support is agriculture, and almost everything is done by hand. There are a lot of work-related injuries in villages like this. And if a person is injured, it is even more difficult to survive. The average worker in this region makes the U.S. equivalent of about $70 per year.

We didn't solve their economic problems or provide them with labor-saving machinery. All we did was cross a line. A powerful, invisible one. For one day—maybe longer—my dad and Norm made a difference in someone's life. As the government escorts told us later, long after the medicine is gone, they will remember that we came to them.

I mentioned in a previous chapter that when we were on the tarmac of the Chengdu airport celebrating the arrival of the cargo plane full of this medicine, a group of children gave us flowers and pictures they had drawn. They crossed a line that day too. We had seen them from a distance and thought that they looked beautiful, but we didn't know why they were there.

Then, when they ran to us, seeking us out individually, thanking us for coming to Chengdu, and giving us these gifts, they crossed traditional lines of age, culture, nationality, and political ideology to say, "I have something for you."

One of our volunteers, Rex Davidson, thanked a little boy for the flowers, but that wasn't enough for the boy. He emphatically motioned for Rex to unroll the picture and look at it. "He wasn't satisfied with just fulfilling the requirement," Rex said. "He wanted me to see what he had done for me. He wanted to connect." When Rex unrolled it and saw that it was a beautiful watercolor, he and the boy hugged, and the boy then ran back to rejoin his group. It didn't matter what any of our pictures looked like, really. What mattered, and what Rex will remember, is that this was the picture someone drew for him. Someone crossed some invisible lines to do this. And well after the pictures are worn, torn, or lost, we will remember that they came to us.

And well after the pictures are worn, torn, or lost, we will remember that they came to us.

When we returned from the mountain towns to Chengdu to get ready to leave China, we got some unfortunate news. One of the key government people from Szechwan, Mr. Yi Jun, had been taken to the hospital while we were gone. It seemed he was going blind in one eye, very suddenly. Surgery was scheduled for the next day.

We were concerned for him because we felt that we knew him. He had been part of the planning of this airlift almost from the beginning. He was the vice director of foreign investment and assistant to the secretary general. He had come to the U.S. to work out final details a few months before. He had been extremely efficient and helpful, coordinating the efforts of the ministries of finance, of health, of transportation. Several of our group noted that he was the best dressed of all of us with his beautiful suits and ever-present leather attaché. We found out about his condition only because he had sent his apologies for not being able to tell us good-bye in person.

Barbi Moore suggested we visit him in the hospital.

At first our escorts seemed reluctant to take a few of us there, but after a few phone calls—to whom I don't know—they said they would take us. We drove into the Southwestern Medical University complex and walked in.

We walked up several flights of stairs to the ophthalmology floor of the hospital and entered a ward that had 10 beds in it. We could hardly fit in the room because it was already so crowded. We saw Mr. Yi in the last bed, on top of the blanket still in his natty suit, with his attaché on the bed against the wall. He looked frightened.

"It all comes down to this," I thought to myself. Here's a man used to fine clothes, police escorts, international travel, and other evidences of an executive lifestyle. Now he's in a damp, noisy, cold room with everyone else. All he's got is his attaché—his papers are his most important possessions.

Barbi took one of his hands, and I took the other. I had been making speeches all day and always had something to say at a moment's notice. But now, I was speechless. It was another one of those magic moments—so poignant, so memorable, so filled with emotion. There wasn't a lot we could say. Not much we needed to say. He got the message, though. We had come. Shown up. Crossed the line. We hadn't brought him an ophthalmology laser to treat him, or a volunteer eye doctor. We were merely present. Finally we told him he was at a good hospital with good doctors, and that we all wanted him to do well in his upcoming surgery. We told him that some of the members of our delegation believed in God, and that they would pray for him. Tears streamed out of the corners of his eyes onto the bed. We were there just a few minutes.

In the car on the way back to the rest of our group, no one said a word. I think it dawned on all of us that, even though we had just brought $6 million in medicine to his country, we had just done something far more important.

In the middle of doing something big—something few peo-

ple get to do—we did something small. Something anyone
could have done. And it was powerful.

That night during our group wrap-up session, the doors to
the conference room opened, and in walked the secretary general. Through his translator he said, "If you can take part of your
day to visit someone from my staff, I can take time tonight to
personally tell you thank you."

Lots of lines getting crossed now.

At this point we were well beyond any calculated public
opinion campaign designed to improve some Americans' views
of China so that those views could influence public policy between the two countries. We were at the level of seeing that, as
human beings who are on opposite sides of the planet, from
countries that sometimes consider each other enemies, we have
more that is similar than dissimilar.

We all had purpose that night, including the secretary general.

Showing Up

There is a lot of power in crossing these lines. I call it the
power of presence. Of showing up.

It is the same power Norm Shoemaker talks about when he
interprets the story of the Good Samaritan. Most people are familiar with the story. It starts with a question from a man looking for life's meaning. "What must I do to inherit eternal life?"
is the same question as "How do I make my life count for something?" or "What is my purpose as a human being?"

The answer, he is told, has already been written. "Love
God and love your neighbor." But the man wants to know exactly to whom he is obligated. So he asks, "Who is my neighbor?" Then he is told this story: A man is traveling and is
stopped by robbers, who beat him and leave him to die along
the road. The first two people who see him lying there walk on
the other side of the road to avoid him. They were both extremely religious people—their religion was their life and liveli-
hood. They were also allies with the victim through their politics, culture, and bloodlines. Yet somehow their religion hadn't
taught them about meeting needs of others.

The man who did stop and help was a Samaritan—a man from a nation considered the enemy to the Jews. This is why it's such a good story. The Samaritan crossed the line of politics, culture, and bloodlines to help someone.

In other words, as Norm would say, the Samaritan showed up. He was present. And he responded. In the power of his presence, the Samaritan saw to it that the man's needs were met.

So the question at the end of the story turns the original question on its head. Instead of "Who is my neighbor?" which is also saying, "Who am I required to look out for?" the question became "Who *acted* like a neighbor?" which is also saying, "This isn't really about others—it's about *me.*"

"Go and do likewise," the man is told (Luke 10:25-37, NIV).

The Samaritan didn't have to go out of his way to find this man. In fact, the religious leaders had to go out of their way to *avoid* him. The needs of others are all around us. We can do something about some of them by just showing up.

Just showing up is all we did at a prison in Russia a few years ago. I had been there before on a trip to see what kind of medicine the people needed. I had left them a business card and said I would be back with something they could use. I didn't realize then that they didn't believe me.

> Just showing up is all we did at a prison in Russia a few years ago.

During an airlift to the region a few months later, a few of us showed up with duffel bags full of medicine and supplies. When the warden saw me, he seemed stunned.

"You came back!" he said.

"Didn't I say I would?" I asked.

Then he reached into his desk and pulled out an enormous stack of business cards.

"All of these people have been here before, too, and said they would come back," he said. "They never have."

That's understandable, I suppose, given the conditions of the place. It was a horrifying facility. Cells designed for maybe a dozen people had at least 75 in them. The stench alone was overpowering.

We gave the prisoners gifts and gave the prison medical staff supplies that they hadn't seen in years.

Just a Few Miles

These sound like major events, but they're really not. There are hospitals and prisons in every town. The lines we cross don't have to be oceans. Sometimes they are the distance of just a few miles.

In an essay written for *Christianity Today* magazine, Philip Yancey tells about his memory of Henri Nouwen. Nouwen's final years were spent at a home for the seriously disabled. He did a lot of speaking and writing, but he lived with people who could not take care of themselves.

Yancey recalled a conversation he had with some famous Christian writers, and the topic was letters they had received from readers. Each had heard from one young man in particular, who asked very intense questions about spiritual growth. All of the writers suggested books and answered the questions as best they could.

"You won't believe what Nouwen did," one of the writers said. "He invited this stranger to live with him for a month so he could mentor him in person."

Henri Nouwen had meaning and significance in his life. He had found his purpose.

During these years Nouwen also cared for Adam, a 26-year-old man who was unable to walk, talk, get dressed, or feed himself. It took Nouwen two hours to prepare Adam for each day. When Yancey asked if there weren't someone else who could do these things for Adam, Nouwen said that Yancey had misunderstood something. "It is *I*, not Adam, who gets the main benefit from our friendship," Nouwen said.

He admitted that, at first, physical touching, showing affection, and dealing with the constant mess was difficult. But over time he said he learned what it must be like for God to love us, "spiritually uncoordinated, retarded, able to respond with what must seem to God like inarticulate grunts and groans."

To paraphrase Mother Teresa once again, we owe the poor a great debt of gratitude for allowing us to become someone of significance.

About four years ago I left my traditional medical practice so I could have more time to be involved in the lives of the poor. I started working for several days in a row in an emergency room at St. Joseph Memorial Hospital in Larned, Kansas, so that I could have concentrated time to devote to Heart to Heart activities.

A lot has changed with my work. The Larned "experiment" took fire and has spread to 35 other hospitals. I turned it into a professional corporation, of which I am the president, called "Docs Who Care." We work in six different states in the Midwest/Mountain region. I still work occasional ER shifts, but I fill in at all the hospitals. I may work a 24-hour shift at one location and then work three days in a row at another location several weeks later.

And while my work with "Docs Who Care" is a means for me to do something more "global," I understand the role of presence in the lives of the people I am treating. I don't ignore them because I am concentrating too much on the needs of refugees in Zaire. On the day of my one-year anniversary with the Larned hospital, the staff gathered in a hospital conference room and presented me with a gift. It was a large, wooden key with the shape of a heart wood-burned into the center. It said, "You hold the key to our hearts." I wondered about that statement later. *I* held the key? How? I had only been there for a year. Even when I am there, it is for just a few days at a time.

I'm interested in them.

I care about them.

They're within my reach, within my ability to love.

I believe this is the reason: I listen to them. I'm interested in them. I care about them. They're within my reach, within my ability to love. I cross the line to go to their homes for meals when I can, whether they're orderlies, nurses, or other doctors. I show up.

In his book *Lines and Shadows,* author Joseph Wambaugh writes about life along the border that separates San Diego from Tijuana, California from Baja California, the United States from Mexico, one of the richest economic forces in the world from one of the poorest. It's just an imaginary line, Wambaugh says. Someone made it up after a war. It wasn't always there. A group of military and political people put it there.

If you happen to be born on one side of the line, your life will be dramatically different from the life you will have if you happen to be born on the other side, Wambaugh writes. It's not because of anything you've done. It's because of the line.

I got to thinking about that imaginary line and realized that most of the lines we confront really are imaginary. Many times they are contrived, driven by a desire for economic or political power, or some other kind of control. Most lines that keep us apart are made by human beings. That means they can be erased by human beings just as easily.

Look at the line that kept the people in that small village from us, or the line that kept us from the children on the tarmac, or the line that kept the Samaritan from the Jew. Invisible lines. Made up. Imaginary.

I have come to a conclusion about these lines: It is a good thing to cross them.

This book is about crossing lines. God crossed one to enter into our lives. That made all other lines irrelevant. The Bible and the life of Jesus make that clear.

Rich or poor, sick or healthy, male or female, third world or first world, Communist or capitalist—the lines that traditionally keep us from being in-

> This book
> is about
> crossing lines.
> God crossed one
> to enter
> into our lives.

volved in each other's lives are more imaginary than real. They are ready for crossing. And until we start moving past them, we'll keep asking the question of why our lives seem empty and meaningless.

I spoke to a group about Heart to Heart, and a man came up to me afterward to tell me that he had tried doing these things I was encouraging members of the audience to do, but he kept running into problems.

He wanted to start a home for teenage mothers. Great idea, I told him. We need more of those. It didn't work out, though, because he couldn't get his city council to approve the purchase of a facility. Then he couldn't raise the $50,000 he thought he needed for start-up money; then he couldn't get a Board of Directors to agree on what exactly the home should be. So he abandoned his idea. Now he's frustrated, discouraged, and not convinced that getting involved in the needs of others is such a good idea after all.

It's time to show up, to be present, to cross the line.

Everything he tried had failed. I told him that, while his desire to help others was noble, his approach would not succeed. Why not start by taking one person into his home and see where that leads?

Mother Teresa didn't wait until she had a Board of Directors before she picked up children and taught them the alphabet, or before she rescued a dying woman from rats and ants and gave her a loving place to spend her last few days.

We didn't wait until we had enough money or staff to do a major medical airlift before we reached out to someone in need. We fixed a community YWCA.

Mike Meyers didn't wait until he had an international company to provide sophisticated medical equipment to Vietnam hospitals before he did something. First he got one instrument.

We don't need any more studies, committees, or think tanks to tell us that people around us are dying. Or that *we* are dying, trying to find meaning in our lives. We've avoided these needs for long enough. It's time to be the one, to go now, to think small, to use your network, to love your enemies, to catch the vision, to find your place, to touch those within your reach, and to celebrate the arrival of meaning in your life.

It's time to show up, to be present, to cross the line.

Stanley Mooneyham asks the question in his book title, *What Do You Say to a Hungry World?* Tony Campolo, in one of his books, asks, "What'cha gonna do with what'cha got?" Jesus asks, "Who acted like the neighbor?"

Now I'm asking, "Are you ready to cross the line?" As soon as you say yes, you'll see that there wasn't much of line there in the first place. A line that might have taken hundreds of years to establish can vanish in seconds. Your heart, your soul, will come alive when you decide to cross the line. And you'll wonder why you waited as long as you did.

APPENDIX

If you want to know more about Heart to Heart International and how you can assist us in our mission to provide help and hope to people in need around the world, please visit our web site at **www.hearttoheart.org**, or E-mail us at **info@hearttoheart.org**. You can also contact one of our offices at:

World Headquarters
Heart to Heart International
401 S. Clairborne, Suite 302
Olathe, KS 66062
Phone: 913-764-5200
Fax: 913-764-0809

Central Regional Office
Heart to Heart International
5915 N.W. 23rd Street, Suite 205
Oklahoma City, OK 73127
Phone: 405-787-5200
Fax: 405-787-5328

Western Regional Office
Heart to Heart International
4005 Camino del Rio South
San Diego, CA 92108
Phone: 619-521-3821
Fax 619-521-3824

YES! I want to get involved in making a difference in my community and around the world!

Name: _____

Company: _____

Address: _____

City: _____ State: _____ Zip: _____

Phone: _____ Fax: _____

E-mail: _____

Thank you for your contact information! We will add your name to our mailing list and keep you updated on our projects in the United States and around the world.

I would like more information about (check all that apply):

☐ Becoming a Heart to Heart Partner through regular giving.

☐ Being a volunteer delegate on a future Heart to Heart airlift.

☐ Volunteering as a part of Heart to Heart's Domestic Program.

☐ Other: _____

Please tear off this bottom section, and mail to our World Headquarters Office (address information above).

REFERENCES

Books

Eiseley, Loren. 1978. *The Star Thrower.* New York: Harcourt Brace and Co.

Lewis, C. S. 1950. *The Lion, The Witch, and the Wardrobe.* New York: Collier Books (A Division of Macmillan Publishing Co.).

Manning, Brennan. 1990. *Ragamuffin Gospel.* Portland, Oreg.: Mulnomah.

Mooneyham, Stanley. 1975. *What Do You Say to a Hungry World?* Waco, Tex.: Word Books.

Muggeridge, Malcolm. 1971. *Something Beautiful for God.* London: Harper and Row.

Nouwen, Henri. 1983. *Compassion.* Garden City, N.Y.: Image Books.

——. 1978, 7th ed. *Out of Solitude.* Notre Dame, Ind.: Ave Maria Press.

——. 1989. *Seeds of Hope.* New York: Bantam Books.

Peck, Scott. 1987. *The Different Drum.* New York: Simon and Schuster.

Magazine Articles

Yancey, Phillip. 1996. "The Holy Inefficiency of Henri Nouwen." *Christianity Today,* December 9, 80.